Text copyright © BRF 2011
The author asserts the moral right
to be identified as the author of this work

Published by
The Bible Reading Fellowship
15 The Chambers, Vineyard
Abingdon OX14 3FE
United Kingdom
Tel: +44 (0)1865 319700
Email: enquiries@brf.org.uk
Website: www.brf.org.uk
BRF is a Registered Charity

ISBN 978 1 84101 827 0
First published 2011
10 9 8 7 6 5 4 3 2 1 0
All rights reserved

Acknowledgments
Unless otherwise stated, scripture quotations are taken from the Holy Bible, New International
Version, copyright © 1973, 1978, 1984 by International Bible Society, are used by permission
of Hodder & Stoughton Publishers, a member of the Hachette Livre Group UK. All rights
reserved. 'NIV' is a registered trademark of International Bible Society. UK trademark number
1448790.

Scripture quotations taken from The Revised Standard Version of the Bible, copyright © 1946,
1952, 1971 by the Division of Christian Education of the National Council of the Churches of
Christ in the United States of America, are used by permission. All rights reserved.

Scripture quotations from THE MESSAGE. Copyright © by Eugene H. Peterson 1993, 1994,
1995. Used by permission of NavPress Publishing Group.

A catalogue record for this book is available from the British Library

Printed in Singapore by Craft Print International Ltd

4Pioneers
Life

**Explorations in theology and wisdom
for pioneering leaders**

edited by David Male

Contents

Contributors

Richard Bauckham is Professor Emeritus in the University of St Andrews and Senior Scholar at Ridley Hall College, Cambridge.

Adrian Chatfield is Director of the Simeon Centre for Prayer and Spiritual Life at Ridley Hall, Cambridge. He is also a member of the Fresh Expressions team with responsibility for prayer and spirituality.

Bishop Graham Cray is the Archbishops' Missioner and leader of the Fresh Expressions team.

John Drane is a mission consultant, co-chair of the Mission Theology Advisory Group and also Professor of Practical Theology at Fuller Seminary in California.

Peterson Feital is originally from Brazil and has been an evangelist for 16 years. He worked as a mission and discipleship adviser for large churches in Brazil and was a Bible lecturer at a Baptist University. He is now training to be an Ordained Pioneer Minister.

Beth Keith is Learning Networks Coordinator for the Fresh Expressions team, developing and supporting learning networks, and works for the Church Army's Sheffield Centre.

George Lings is the Director of The Sheffield Centre, Church Army's research unit into fresh expressions of church and church planting.

David Male is the Director of the Centre for Pioneer Learning in Cambridge and teaches pioneers in training at Ridley Hall and Westcott House in Cambridge. Previously he was part of the team that planted the Net Church in Huddersfield.

Kate Middleton is a psychologist and was Director of Anorexia and Bulimia Care. She is now Director of Care at Hitchin Christian Centre.

Lucy Moore works for BRF as Messy Church Team Leader. She is responsible for developing the work of Messy Church® nationally and internationally—writing, speaking, reflecting and developing Messy projects.

Mike Moynagh is based at Wycliffe Hall, Oxford, works for Fresh Expressions as editor of Share and has a watching brief for the education and training of Ordained Pioneer Ministers. He is also co-director of the Tomorrow Project, which advises businesses and government on social trends.

Mark Russell is the Chief Executive of Church Army. He is a member of the Archbishops' Council and General Synod of the Church of England.

Introduction

I am a pioneer who has a real passion to encourage, network, develop and sustain all types of pioneers. It is exciting to be part of a church that is rediscovering the role of the pioneer for our new missionary situation. It has been amazing to see how the role of Lay and Ordained Pioneer Ministers has developed in the Church of England alongside the Methodist Venture FX. Other denominations are doing similar things, even though they may not use exactly the same language. Training courses for pioneers, like the Misson-Shaped Ministry course and ReSource, are springing up. Everywhere I go, people want to think about what it means to be, discover or train a pioneering leader. I think we are only at the beginning of our explorations about what it means to be a pioneer and what it means for the church to have pioneers, and I hope this book will help in taking the debate further.

The issue of what we mean by the word 'pioneer' is a subject with which George Lings grapples in this book—and of course we do not want to limit the readership of this book only to those with 'pioneer' somewhere in their job title. It is for anyone in a pioneering leadership role who is breaking new ground for the sake of God's gospel. It is a book for lay and ordained people from a variety of church backgrounds.

Pioneers 4 Life is a product of our Breakout Pioneers Conference (www.breakoutpioneer.org.uk), an annual three-day gathering of pioneers, both lay and ordained, from across the denominations. All the monies from this book will go to help with the finances of future conferences. Many of the chapters have been delivered at the conference and the pioneer stories are from people who attend the gathering. We have tried, in the selection of the contributors, to reflect a real diversity, to help us think about all the facets of pioneering. As you read these chapters, you will find many points of unity but also some important areas of disagreement. It is important that we learn from various disciplines, so here we have some great mission thinkers such as John Drane and George Lings, key practitioners such as Lucy Moore, eminent theologians such as Richard Bauckham, and those who are shaping church policy, such as Graham Cray and Mark Russell. The views that the authors share are their personal views and do not necessarily reflect the views of the organisations they work for.

As editor, it has been exciting for me to read their contributions, which have been thought-provoking, practical and encouraging. It has been interesting to see how similar themes have emerged in different chapters and how often they build on and interact with each other. Some of the contributions are more theological and some more practical, but together they create a substantial help for pioneers, those working with pioneers, commentators and thinkers and those who are permission givers. I don't think any of us authors would claim to have the definitive word on any of these issues. We are all learners together, but some very useful questions and some tentative answers have been sketched out.

The role of pioneers is going to be vital if we are truly to be a church that reaches everyone in our society. We are struggling to know how to connect with those who are way outside the orbit of the church, but I suspect and hope that pioneers will be the bridgeheads into new places. In the light of this, I have identified six key issues emerging from this book.

Pioneers realise the need to pioneer pioneering

We cannot and should not remove ourselves from the rest of the church, but we must work at developing our role in order to make the journey easier for the next generation of pioneers. We need to be involved in the way pioneers are discovered, formed, trained, deployed, employed and supported. We must help to create good patterns of work that will allow others to follow on and develop what we have done. It is important that our voices are heard constructively and that we are not only shaping our own projects but also shaping the church of the present and the future.

We must move on from here

Although pioneering has made a good start, we need to recognise that (as mentioned already) missionally we are struggling to connect with large areas of our society. There is a danger in only going so far, staying in safe waters, not venturing too deep. I think we are being called to set out into the deep, and there will be no return to what has been before. Things are changing so dramatically in our society that we cannot simply change to being a trendier church; we need to become more revolutionary in our thinking about what future forms of church may look like—forms that stay loyal to Christ but are radical in expression. We need to pull up the anchor and set sail, trusting God for where we may go.

This also means that the church needs to release its pioneers. The danger is that pioneers are required to be like any other Christian leader, but doing a bit of pioneering on the side. Instead, they must be allowed to fulfil their calling and, like the apostle Philip (Acts 8:26–40), to go where the Spirit takes them. Please don't squash the life out of them by trying to fit them into old models that do not relate to their calling!

Both imagination and permission are needed

It is not enough simply to imagine what the future might look like; we also need those in authority to give permission for changes to happen. Those two elements together are very powerful, but they require a church that is willing to take risks. We are unable to guarantee the future and not everything will be successful, but that does not mean we should not try. Those things that do not work immediately may become important prototypes for what might be in the future.

We must come together

It is really important that pioneers find places and spaces to meet with each other, to find support, renewal and encouragement. I have loved being part of various pioneer networks where I can be myself and do not have to defend or endlessly explain what I am trying to do.

We need many more pioneers

I still worry that many of our models of leadership are educated, male, white and ordained. Yet it is often the clergy person in a fresh expression of church who is the big financial drain, otherwise it would hardly cost anything to develop such a new church. The future of pioneering must lie with lay people. We need to find a way to focus our training and development on them. We don't need just a few fresh expressions; we need thousands, up and down the country, which inhabit all the various cultures of our society. We need to invest in people who have the ability to develop tent-making ministries and social enterprises as part of their pioneering. We need to do whatever it takes at a national and local level for people to see and hear the gospel in their locality.

The next generation is important

I do not think that most of those who are present pioneers are the key people for the future. I believe the most important pioneers will be the next generation, who came to faith from unchurched backgrounds in a fresh expression of church. They will not have the baggage carried by those of us who have been in the church for some time. They are the people who will take us into new areas and create churches that we have not yet even imagined. I think our biggest present task is to find these next-generation pioneers, nurture and support them, and train them in such a way that they are free to pioneer as God leads them, not just in the ways we have always done it. They may hold the key to the future; our most pressing need is to ensure that they have the opportunities to fulfil their calling.

Thank you so much to anyone who is reading this and pioneering something. Thank you for taking the risk—for your faith, commitment, sacrifice and boldness. We need you and we need a church that appreciates you deeply. I would also like to express my sincere thanks to all the contributors who have given much effort and time to produce such great work. Thank you to the group who organise the Breakout Conference with me, to Church Army, Fresh Expressions and FX Venture, who sponsored it, and to all those who attend the conference. Thanks, Annette, for the coffee. The conference is always a highlight of my year.

Thanks to Naomi Starkey, our editor, for her work in sorting out our mess, and also to everybody who has helped me in the recent forming of the Centre for Pioneer Learning in Cambridge. A special thanks to George Lings, who has been my mentor for many years and has given me time, encouraged me and taught me so much. But above all, thanks to Heather, my wife, for her continual support, love and patience.

1

Thus far and much further: the contemporary scene

Graham Cray

At the time of writing, I am one year into my role as Archbishops' Missioner and Leader of the Fresh Expressions team. The second phase of the team's work is well under way, and it is a good time to take stock.

In February 2004 it was my privilege to present the *Mission-Shaped Church* report to General Synod, having little idea of the scale of the response, which would follow. The working party had prayed that we would present a report 'of' the Church of England, in which it could recognise itself, rather than 'at' the Church of England—with a bunch of radicals telling our church what to do. That prayer was answered beyond our imagination (or faith!). The events of the last six years have convinced me that we are involved, in part at least, in a movement initiated by the Holy Spirit. We seem to have caught or been caught up by a wave of the Spirit, and our central task is not to fall off.

One significant piece of evidence in support of this is the ecumenical nature of the work. From the beginning, the Fresh Expressions initiative has been a full partnership between the

Church of England and the Methodist Connexion. The level of cooperation has been admirable and together we have given some substance to our Covenant. Since then, both the Congregational Federation and the United Reformed Church have become partners. In Scotland we work closely with the Church of Scotland. But locally, when we offer training, there is often a wider range of Christian traditions involved. In Kent, for example, the Mission-Shaped Ministry course has been Anglican, Methodist, URC, Baptist and Salvation Army from the beginning. These days, it seems, mission is the driver for the most motivated expressions of local ecumenism. We unite locally for the sake of others, and, for their sakes, we address a shared weakness: the ineffectiveness of many of our historic approaches to mission to engage with many parts of our current society. It is fitting that the other formal partners in Fresh Expressions are all mission agencies or missional movements: Church Army, Church Mission Society (CMS) and Anglican Church Planting Initiatives (ACPI).

This chapter, however, is about the progress made in establishing fresh expressions of church across the country, not primarily about the national team. One of the most impressive developments has been the sheer range of fresh expressions.[1] I want to pay tribute to the hundreds of lay leaders and clergy who have launched imaginative initiatives among their neighbourhoods and networks over the last few years.[2] They can be found in rural and urban settings, among new housing developments and cathedral cities, in suburban and city centre parishes. Every churchmanship is represented: Traditional and Affirming Catholic, Conservative and Open Evangelical, New Wine churches, middle-of-the-road churchmanship, contemplative communities and the majority of parishes, circuits and synods where no one tradition predominates.

The more unusual examples—located in farmers' markets and skate parks or focused on mountain bikers or surfers (a notable Methodist example!)—get the media attention, but the great majority are fledgling congregations, meeting at a convenient time and in a welcoming place, and are well within the capability of the average church. A wide range of examples can be found on the Fresh Expressions and Share websites (see www.freshexpressions. org.uk/stories and www.sharetheguide.org/examples).

Despite the obvious popularity and value of certain models—Messy Church, Café Church and so on—the sheer range of projects is highly impressive, to the extent that when the *Methodist Recorder* published a good-natured 1st April spoof about 'Knitting Church', they discovered to their chagrin that there was a real-life excellent example, called Loving Hands, and it was Methodist!

I am aware of only a handful of fresh expressions ministering among ethnic minorities. This is a challenge for the future, particularly in our cities, and I believe we will only progress as we develop new partnerships. I was pleased to attend the Archbishop of Canterbury's consultation with leaders of 'Black Majority' churches. It was moving to hear brothers and sisters, whose forefathers had come to faith through our forefathers' missionary sacrifice, share their calling to come to this nation for the same gospel purpose. Many of these churches thrive among their own peers but, like us, often struggle to evangelise cross-culturally. We have much to learn from one another, and I pray that new partnerships will develop.

In our training courses, we teach that the mission of the church is to participate in the mission of God: 'seeing what God is doing and joining in'. As I have reflected on the story so far, a combination of three factors has been crucial to the progress made. First, there is a new imagination about the form or shape of church. Christians are imagining the possibility of new forms of church for the sake of mission. Second, there is a new era of permission and encouragement by church leaders. In Church of England terms, the statement that has put an end to many a bright idea, 'The bishop would never allow it', has, in many dioceses, become 'The bishop would be most disappointed if you did not try.' Finally, there have been training resources, many provided by the Fresh Expressions team. These three factors combine in a dynamic ecology. Churches can imagine appropriate fresh expressions of church; they are not just permitted but encouraged to take the risk of starting one; and training is available to show them how.

A number of issues have emerged along the way. The first is the need to provide some discipline and coherence to the terminology. An inevitable consequence of a high-profile initiative is that the use of its distinctive language becomes elastic. Lately, it has been almost impossible to attempt anything new, in the partner denominations, without calling it a 'fresh expression' of something, or 'mission-shaped'. There has also been some rebranding of existing work and some consumer church planting, which was more for the sake of the planters' preferences than contextual for others. My desire in bringing some discipline to the vocabulary is not to define good work out of recognition or to discredit good pieces of mission and ministry, but to make clear the heart of the terminology.

A 'fresh expression' is shorthand for 'a fresh expression of church'. Our task is to encourage the planting of new congregations or churches among those untouched by existing churches. We contrast that task with initiatives to draw people into existing congregations, not because we disapprove (on the contrary, that is an essential part of any church's mission) but because it is not what the terminology from *Mission-Shaped Church* means.

'Fresh' is not the opposite of 'stale'. Nor is a fresh expression of church to be defined as the opposite of inherited or traditional (although it is meant to be complementary to it). *Mission-Shaped Church* is an Anglican document, and 'fresh' is rooted in the Declaration of Assent that all clergy make on their ordination and, subsequently, each time they are licensed to a new post. According to this declaration, 'the faith uniquely revealed in the Holy Scriptures and set forth in the catholic creeds, to which the Church of England has borne witness in its historic formularies' has to be 'proclaimed afresh in each generation', and the minister promises to draw on these historic resources to 'bring the grace and truth of

Christ to this generation'. Our understanding is that, today, that proclamation often involves a fresh embodiment of the gospel in new, contextually appropriate communities of faith—fresh expressions of church, as fresh embodiments of the faith, among a community of people who had not known it or had lost touch with the church.

As we have observed and participated in these developments, we have identified a process, as a form of best practice. Many fresh expressions of church begin with a period of listening to God and to the relevant community. *Mission-Shaped Church* calls this 'double listening'. They develop through consistent patterns of service, building the relationships through which a community can form around Christ. In these relationships, evangelism can have its proper place and discipleship be explored. An appropriate pattern of worship and sacramental life can then emerge, in which new and restored believers, and those on the way to clearer faith, can play a full part.

The planting team may have seen such relationships as church from the beginning. For those being drawn into faith, there will be a growing understanding of what it means to be church. Meanwhile, denominational authorities offer encouragement and support to the embryonic church from the beginning, but properly delay permanent recognition until there is evidence of stability.

Fresh expressions of church are contextual: they are to be appropriate to the local or intended context. They require a costly incarnational approach, which prioritises the needs of the neighbourhood or network over the preferences of the planting team. In *Mission-Shaped Church* we called this approach 'dying to live'. Discernment in context becomes the crucial capacity— again, 'seeing what God is doing and joining in'. These are to be communities for the kingdom, not just about the expansion of the church. Many are birthed through acts of service. The commitment to an incarnational approach is to ensure that they can become transformational communities for their wider community, rather than existing purely for themselves or being inculturated in a (to them) alien church culture.

Because many fresh expressions of church are still fledgling Christian communities, this is a young movement and there is still a great deal to learn about sustainability. Which communities are properly seasonal rather than long-term? Which have the capacity to become longstanding and mature congregations? How long before they become self-supporting, while at the same time remaining properly interdependent with other local congregations and churches? How quickly can indigenous leadership be developed? Can the cross-cultural and incarnational gene be passed on, so that a fresh expression plants a new fresh expression, to reach a different part of our culturally complex mission field? We are inevitably very early in this particular learning curve, but it will be a vital focus for the whole movement in the coming years.

If fresh expressions of church are to mature and to be properly interconnected, they will need appropriate local support. We are encouraging the development of FEASTs (not as exciting as it sounds: Fresh Expressions Area Strategy Teams) in each area. These are ecumenical teams of senior leaders, advocates, trainers and experienced practitioners whose task is to nurture the development of fresh expressions of church and pioneer ministry in their region, and to sponsor training.

All that I have been saying needs to be put in the context of the 'mixed economy' church. The language of the mixed economy is not simply a device to create space and permission for fresh expressions of church to coexist with more inherited approaches. Catholicity requires both diversity and interdependence. The mixed economy demonstrates a dynamic partnership, a context in which inherited church has encouraged, and often funded, fresh expressions initiatives, and where the planting of a fresh expression of church has in turn brought renewal and encouragement to a more traditional congregation. There is potential for all sorts of grace-filled giving and receiving.

The sheer scale of progress over the last six years has been breathtaking and is a matter for great thankfulness to God. We have come a long way fast; but we should not fool ourselves about the distance still to be travelled.

It is clear that many fresh expressions of church have re-engaged with a fringe, which no longer exists to the scale it did in previous generations. This has been done through the establishing of new congregations or through the transformation of existing pieces of community ministry into new congregations. (Many of those working with young families, for example, have used BRF's excellent *Messy Church* material.) This has been a challenging task for many parishes and is precisely the degree of progress we could realistically have expected from the first years of this initiative. Many churches have done well. But most fresh expressions still only reach dechurched people, or people who are immediately open to considering an invitation to an event. We have to go much further.

The Tearfund survey of church attendance, published in 2007, shows that the largest group of adults (that is, aged 16 and over) in England are those who have never had more than a fleeting contact with any Christian church in their lifetime. They amount to 34 per cent. The next largest category is the dechurched, amounting to another 31 per cent. Our churches have had wide open back doors for years and we have not done enough to enquire why so many have gone through them and never returned. In *Mission-Shaped Church*, based on research for the mid-1990s, the dechurched category divided equally between those who were open to return and those who were closed. Ten years later, the proportions are five-sixths closed, and only one-sixth open to return. This is why fresh expressions of church, beyond this fringe, are so important for the future of the Church's ministry. Many children of the dechurched become the next generation of never-churched; and if we were to add the under-16s to complete the national picture, the never-churched might be the majority of the population. In addition, there is an age disparity. The average Church of England worshipper is nearly 14 years older than the average age of the population.

Most local churches, or groups of small churches, have the potential to plant a fresh expression of church. We have done well, but we can do much more. The mixed economy needs to be the norm, not the activity of an enterprising few.

There are major advantages in working ecumenically, through local Churches Together groups and through churches working together under the Hope (formerly Hope 08) banner. A light-touch ecumenical procedure that does not automatically progress to a Local Ecumenical Project is urgently needed to facilitate local partnership.

To engage with those who have no knowledge of the faith, and no apparent need of the Church, takes time. We are challenged to a long-term incarnational ministry. The gradual separation of the church from the lives of so many has taken decades and the tide will not be turned quickly. This has financial consequences. It is already clear that three-year funded projects are not adequate and that there is no quick fix. Church Army experience says, 'Plan for a ten-year project and review after five.'

There will, I believe, be an increasing role for pioneer ministers, both lay and ordained. This is not to say that other clergy have no capacity for pioneering work. All ministers will need a more entrepreneurial approach if our effective mission field is not to age and shrink further. I have been involved in the Church of England's Ordained Pioneer Minister scheme from the beginning. At the time of writing, 90 people have been recommended for training and many of them are deployed. In addition, some dioceses have recognised the pioneering skills of those who were ordained before this pathway was possible.

As a result of the last five years' experience, we have been able to revise the selection criteria and introduce a new selection process. The revision process drew also on Church Army and CMS experience. It is now possible for candidates for assistant or local ministry to be designated pioneer, not just those of incumbent capacity—a move that should enable vocations for ordination from within fresh expressions. The revised selection process will assess candidates' capacity and call to pioneering before they attend a Bishops' Advisory Panel.

The strategic deployment of stipendiary Pioneer Ministers is a crucial resource for the future, but we need to deploy far more lay and ordained pioneer ministers than we can possibly afford to employ. Much pioneer church and fresh expression planting will have to be either self-supporting or resourced in new ways. The churches need to learn how to sustain 'tent-making' church planters—like St Paul. A portfolio of practical means of support should be developed in each diocese, district or synod. We need a whole new understanding and culture of self-supporting ministry for mission. Self-supporting cannot be allowed to mean 'left to sink or swim'. The absence of a salary or stipend cannot mean that those who authorise or license pioneers have no responsibility for them, otherwise projects will fail and pioneers be damaged. Pioneers are most vulnerable when they are isolated, particularly when they are not part of a planting team. All pioneers should be in some form of action learning network with others. Those who are planting something new and initially frail need to be part of a larger network.

Fledgling projects and potential pioneers are emerging all over the UK. I recommend that each diocese, district or synod develop a culture of provisional recognition of lay pioneers and new initiatives. In the early stages, there needs to be enough recognition to give each project the best chance to thrive, but leaving formal recognition, where it is needed, until there is evidence of longer-term effective ministry.

We need pioneers because we are facing the long haul rather than toying with the latest fad. A very able pioneer minister said to me recently, 'It's hard work. And it takes for ever. But sometimes you see flashes of God at work, which keeps you going.'

This emphasis on full-time pioneers, whether lay or ordained, is not intended to evade the fact that most fresh expressions of church are likely to be lay-led. The sheer scale of the task requires it. One of the most encouraging features of the last six years has been to see the emergence of a considerable number of lay Christians who are involved in a fresh expression in the middle of busy lives. This missional call and opportunity has released energy and imagination among Christians who were not so energised by being asked to maintain their congregation's status quo.

Looking ahead, the primary question that motivates me is, 'Who will our current forms of church never reach?' As a church we have a responsibility before God for those who do not yet know him: Paul described himself as 'in debt' to them (Romans 1:14–15).

The future has to be multifaceted. The priority is to learn how to engage with the never-churched and plant contextually appropriate fresh expressions among them. This will involve us all in an ongoing commitment to train and envision many congregations who have not yet engaged with the challenge. Just because we have new things to learn, it does not mean that we stop teaching first principles to those who have not been involved thus far. But in this phase of the work, we also have to learn, from practice, how to take fresh expressions of church on to maturity. If fresh expressions of church are contextual, we need skills in the development of 'liturgy from below'—patterns of prayer and worship that are truly the work of the people but also recognisably in the Christian tradition. No expression of church is worthy of the name if it does not eventually develop a sacramental life. Our concern is with deep church in the right place, not church-lite! Baptism, the renewal of baptismal vows, or confirmation should be celebrated in the normal context and ethos of the fresh expression, as a celebration of its ministry. Once an appetite for and understanding of the Eucharist is in place, denominations will need imaginative thinking to ensure that it can legally become part of the rhythm of a fresh expression's life.

Perhaps the greatest challenge facing the church in the West is the question of discipleship. The ultimate test of any church's ministry, whether traditional or a fresh expression, is the quality of the disciples it makes. In the chairman's introduction to *Mission-Shaped Church*, I wrote, 'The gospel has to be heard within the culture of the day, but it always has to be heard as a call to appropriate repentance. It is the incarnation of the gospel, within a dominantly consumer society, that provides the Church of England with its major missionary challenge.'[3] I remain convinced that we have not yet learnt how to make an adequate response to that challenge, but a number of things are clear. First, if the call to discipleship is not within the DNA and intention of the fresh expression from the beginning, it is very difficult to add it in or bolt it on later. The church in the UK tends to isolate evangelism from the call to whole-life, lifelong discipleship. Second, growth in discipleship involves the formation of character through habit. It may be that some form of mutually encouraged rule of life will be necessary. Those fresh expressions of church that draw on new monasticism may have an advantage. Third, the development of indigenous leadership is a key priority. Whatever neighbourhood, network or other group the fresh expression is designed to reach, it is when people from within it begin to ask the questions of daily discipleship and take the initiative among their friends that significant progress can be made. Our task is to equip people for their world, not inculturate them into ours.

Over the last decade or so, the church in the UK has been waking up to the demise of Christendom. It has had to recognise that it will soon be 'no more than the Cheshire cat's grin'.[4] It will take more than the current generation of practitioners to bridge the gap between church and culture. Those of us who are active in the task need also to invest in the next generation. The tiny proportion of young adults who are active in church has to be a matter of focused missionary concern, but we also need to age-proof our inheritance. It would be a tragedy if the lessons learned about discernment in context and about contextual church planting were to be lost because middle-aged practitioners and trainers don't know how to speak 'young adult'. We need to leave behind us an inheritance on which the next generation can build.

Our faith is being proclaimed and embodied afresh: much of the church is learning to be missional. In a few years we have achieved more than I could have imagined, but there is still much, much more to do. I would say, so far so good, thus far, but there is still much further to go and much more to do.

Notes

1 The exact number of fresh expressions is notoriously difficult to count, because of the difficulty of definition, but a recent official survey by the Methodist Church identified nearly 1000 Methodist fresh expressions of church.

2 *Mission-Shaped Church* (CHP, 2004), p. xii.

3 *Mission-Shaped Church*, p. xii.

4 John Finney, *Recovering the Past Celtic and Roman Mission* (DLT, 1996), p. vii.

A pioneer's story

I never quite fitted the mould at theological college: my placements varied from a large charismatic church to a police chaplaincy and Christian outdoor pursuits centres. By the grace of God and a very wise tutor, I realised that not fitting the mould might be a gift, so I rather boldly turned down a few safe curacies and ended up in a great town-centre church where the vicar gave me the permission to experiment and pioneer (although I wouldn't have recognised the title).

As I was nearing the end of my curacy, the Bishop approached me with the suggestion of taking on a three-parish benefice and starting a church plant in a new housing area called Grange Park. Even though I knew practically nothing about planting, I realised that this was an impossible task and turned it down, only to be recalled and offered the plant alone. So I began busily recruiting a team from the church at which I was doing my curacy.

The initial vision was not so much a fresh expression—more of a family-oriented cell church with big and small wings (Sunday service and small groups). 'A New Church for a New Community' we called ourselves, aiming to be connected with people whom the local churches and chapels didn't reach.

The team

We started with 34 people—adults and children—and they worked their socks off running cell groups, services, kids' groups and community outreach. Their commitment and energy were fantastic; the fact that few lived on Grange Park itself didn't seem much of a problem at the time but, if I were to start all over again, I would strongly encourage people to move into the area. There were growing tensions between those who lived in Grange Park and those who travelled in to run events, services or cell groups. My wife Charlotte and I, with our four kids, had moved in and had given ourselves to integrating and being good news to the residents, to some extent at the expense of the hardworking, faithful team from outside. Understandably, a trickle of them, feeling unappreciated, started to leave. If I had communicated a clearer sense of the vision —particularly the focus on Grange Park residents and the fact that the new church would be primarily a church for them, not the dream church of the planting team members—perhaps things may have been easier.

Seven years on, only Richard and his two sons remain from the starting team (other than my own family). While some have moved for ordination training, missionary or youth work, quite a number left under a bit of a cloud: their expressed reasons were varied but underlying them was the fact that this was not the church they had hoped it would become.

Community building

A few years ago, the Evangelical Alliance ran a campaign asking 'If your church vanished overnight, would anyone notice?' This challenge struck a chord in me, and engaging with and building up the local community has been a motif of Grange Park Church over the years. It all started when we ran an event to publicise and launch our first Sunday service. There being, as yet, no actual community building, we decided to set up camp in a square by the playground. With a series of borrowed gazebos as zones for games, crafts, refreshments and so on, we invited the kids and parents to a free event in the last week of the summer holidays. Our dream that they would all flock to Sunday services was a little too optimistic, but a conversation was overheard between two mums who realised that they lived round the corner from each other, had kids of similar ages and then agreed to meet at the park later; this sparked the idea that we were being used by God to connect people together.

Choices, choices

Once you start to get involved in a community, the biggest problem is which of the dozens of worthy causes to support. After a call from a health visitor about the large number of young mums struggling alone with their new offspring, we sensed God's call to start Talking Point, a weekly group in our own home for new mums and babies, with the health visitor dropping in for weighing and advice. It proved a runaway success, not just in helping the mums but in building up community networks and in establishing the church's reputation as being a good thing locally. I can't emphasise enough the principle that 'God-timed' initiatives reap huge rewards. The knack is listening hard to God, and that takes time and effort!

Investing in the few

As the church grew, people came to faith, and as things got busier, I found it very difficult to make the leadership transition from nurturing everyone to focusing on a few. Traces of a 'please everyone' streak remain in me, and I've often found myself spreading myself very thin and promising support and help I never manage to deliver. Playing the long game of focusing attention and energy on a few emerging leaders is the Jesus way and is also more sustainable for the leader.

Money and sustainability

Take whoever holds your purse strings out to lunch once a year and talk money with them. I have been very aware that my diocese took a big risk by funding Grange Park Church, and I want them to think it so worthwhile that they will fund many more fresh expressions and church plants.

Looking after Number One

Without some wise people around me who were prepared to challenge my working patterns, I would not have made it this far. Despite making great improvements in my work–life balance, through the CPAS Arrow Leadership programme and some wise mentoring, I still had to take an extra four weeks off, as I was nearing burnout. Even as I write, I am tired. My wife and I sometimes catch ourselves saying, 'When we do this again…' but at the moment I think I would need a year out to recover enough to start over again.

Passion

Despite the weariness, my passion remains—passion for Jesus, passion to see his kingdom come and his will done in our towns and cities. It's all about him. Find what feeds that passion in you and go to conferences, retreats or whatever sets you on fire again for Jesus.

Charlie Nobbs, an Anglican Minister, has been developing a pioneering church on a new housing estate at Grange Park, Northampton (by the M1 junction 15), for the last seven years.

2

Looking in the mirror: what makes a pioneer?

George Lings

We all make some assumptions when we write. They arise from our distilled view of the past, its interaction with our more recent experiences, and our hopes for the future.

The assumptions I bring

I bring some satisfaction that Recommendation 11 of *Mission-Shaped Church*[1] has led to the recognition within the Church of England that there are such people as pioneers,[2] and that their training and deployment needs are overlapping with, yet different from, the patterns we have known. However, I guessed as soon I heard of these encouraging developments that it would be easier to spot pioneers than to train them differently, and that to deploy them appropriately, within a lifetime's vocational path as pioneers, would be the most difficult of all. I am trying hard now not to say, 'I told you so.' I am concerned that many in the Church of England still think this is an idealistic phase that so-called 'pioneers' will go through, but that realism will eventually arrive and they will settle down to become team vicars and incumbents of existing parishes, having worked the pioneer bug out of their systems. It remains to be seen, in the long term, whether the Methodist Venture FX scheme will prove to be free of this bias.

I also think, from watching people, that the range from pioneering to traditional ministries (all of which might be lay or ordained) is a wide spectrum. At one end I see the pioneer-starters, who are brilliant at initiating things but get bored quickly and need to know when to move on, before they start to destroy what has begun. Then come what I term the pioneer-sustainers. They can not only begin things, but are good at seeing them mature and enable the flourishing of indigenous leadership. Next are some ministers that I call sustainer-innovators, who, despite being traditionally trained, are nevertheless gifted to bring to birth new ventures within an existing church. At the far end, there are other ministers, whom I'd label sustainer-developers, whose gifts are in the effective mainten-ance or slow evolution of what already exists. I believe we need them all, and so I am reserving the 'pioneer' term for originators of fresh entities. However, we need clarity to spot which is which and to devise different timescales and patterns for each. It will also be helpful to practise the principle that all leadership in mission is plural, as it seems to have been in the New Testament from Luke 10 onwards (in which two is the minimum number of people in a partnership). Then the gifts and characteristics needed in missional ministry may be found across a whole team, not just in an individual (such as the person sent from the wider Church).

It also seems to me very plausible that scripture—especially the New Testament, because of its centrifugal mission—contains insights about and examples of pioneers. One example would be the Ephesians 4 list of ministries in which, arguably, the pioneer roles are the apostolic, prophetic and evangelistic ones and the sustainer roles are more akin to the pastor/teacher functions. I find this a more helpful model than the sub-apostolic threefold order of ministry, which I do not accept as a non-negotiable, God-given feature of the universal Church. I see the threefold scheme, rather, as coming from a historical context in which the itinerant dimensions of ministry were fading and the first cross-cultural journey from a Jewish to a Greco-Roman world had occurred. The scheme is thus painted in sustainer colours already, although with positive values of its own.

A connection between pioneer and apostle

Archêgos is sometimes translated in the RSV as 'pioneer' (see Hebrews 2:10; 12:2). The Greek word itself is said to cover meanings like founder, originator and author, even prince or leader.[3] When it is applied to Jesus, he is termed 'the author of life' in Acts 3:15, 'leader and saviour' in Acts 5:31, and 'the pioneer' of our salvation, and of our faith, in Hebrews 12:2. It is the latter epistle that also calls Jesus an apostle (Hebrews 3:1). Some connection between the terms 'pioneer' and 'apostle' is therefore suggested, in which the meanings overlap but are not identical. The difference between the two may be this: 'apostle' is a term derived from a Greek verb meaning 'to send'. It relates to whom the sent person comes from, and what they therefore bring with them, while 'pioneer' describes more of an initiating role, determining both where people go and what they will achieve.

Our recognition of Jesus as apostolic is founded on more than just Hebrews 3:1, of course. It is prominent in his self-description as the 'sent one' in John's Gospel, who also, in turn, 'sends' his followers.[4] Here is the outline of a case for exploring pioneer identity through its links with the apostolic role and with the recognition that Jesus' roles created normative patterns of Christian ministry (with the vital exception that he has unique functions related to his divinity and saving efficacy).

Some key characteristics of the pioneer

Pioneers are the first

With admitted irony, I want to argue that, firstly, pioneers are all about being the first to do or see something.[5] Thus, Einstein could be called the pioneer of the theory of relativity, and Jesus is justifiably called the pioneer of our salvation. He was the first to open the Holy of Holies once for all, taking in his own blood as the sacrifice (Hebrews 9:12). Equally diagnostic and significant is the Christian claim that by Jesus came the resurrection from the dead (1 Corinthians 15:21)—hence we talk about Jesus as the firstborn from the dead (Colossians 1:18).

Being the first is linked to the associated vocabulary of leadership, for although 'first' can refer to simple chronology, as in 'he was first to finish the exam', it also can refer to the first in superiority, as in 'she was first in the exam results'. The latter is usually the more significant but, in a race, the two meanings coincide. It can also be used about practical priority, as in the immortal phrase 'women and children first'. In Hebrews, the description of Jesus as the first is about both superiority and chronology, but the originating function is more important, so some translations of Hebrews 12:1 employ the term 'author' of salvation.

Pioneers are on the edge

Pioneering is not about novelty for its own sake; it is about seeing something that needs to be thought or done, and being the first in a particular context to make it happen. This connects with one contemporary definition of a related figure—the entrepreneur—who, while not identical with the pioneer, at least overlaps with the pioneer's role, being 'a person who habitually creates and innovates to build something of recognised value around perceived opportunities'.[6] The words 'create' and 'innovate' are intrinsically related to being 'first'. Bolton and Thompson later assert, 'Creativity and innovation are the distinguishing marks of the entrepreneur.'[7] Pioneers, following the overall flow of this argument, thus by definition go to the edge and push the boundary, either of what is known or of what has been done before. Often, in ministry, that activity will be relative to context, not absolute. Starting a church community is not novel, though in some places it may be the first one, or it may be the first time it has been done in a particular way. This is related to the reasons why the nuances of the term 'fresh' are preferable to the vexing word 'new'.

Pioneers are followable

Being first and either coming or, better, being sent as leaders, pioneers draw followers.[8] There is no point in being a pioneer that no one can follow. It is apposite, in this connection, that Jesus said, 'Follow me' (the term appears about half a dozen times in each Gospel). Paul then dares to say, 'Imitate me' (2 Thessalonians 3: 7–9; 1 Corinthians 4:16; 11:1).

Those who follow do so in several senses. First, they follow a family pattern laid down. Paul chooses the image of a father and children in the faith, creating a pattern that has been set (1 Corinthians 4:15–17). Today we might talk about inheriting a spiritual DNA. Most importantly for pioneers, there are new followers who used not to be so. In terms of 1 Corinthians 4, they are new children in the faith, and they are described as the seal of Paul's apostleship (1 Corinthians 9:2).[9] Followers also, later, provide resources to consolidate the ground gained, and they provide continuity into the future, after the pioneer has moved on. In this sense they follow on and some become the next leaders. We see this wide pattern with Jesus and then with Paul—which leads us to the next characteristic of pioneers.

Pioneers leave

Pioneers move on when the task is done. Jesus (in John 16) and Paul (in Romans 15) share something of this feature. Jesus goes as far as to say that it is to the disciples' advantage if he goes away (John 16:7). Paul, keen not to build on another's foundation, says that he 'no longer has any room for work in these regions' (Romans 15:23). The pioneering has been done; the 'first' stage has been completed. Yet neither Jesus nor Paul is abandoning those who follow, as a result of boredom or itchy feet; in both cases, they have trained and set in place the right people to act as successors. It is characteristic of pioneers that they are first in and also first out. The appropriate prominence of leaving is echoed by Vincent Donovan: 'The final missionary step as regards the people of any nation or culture, and the most important lesson we will ever teach them—is to leave them.'[10]

Expanding the characteristics

Pioneers are movers

If we accept some overlap between pioneering and being apostolic, and if the latter is linked to being sent, then a sense of authorised movement is to be expected.[11] The words 'pioneer' and 'static' simply do not go together. Thus we may say that the pioneer calling, as we see with Paul in Romans 15, is more to disperse church than to gather it. So, today, pioneers will be those who plant new Christian communities, cross boundaries (whether they be cultural or ecclesial) and occupy new ground. This sense of being called and sent was one basis for the security and identity of an apostle, and is in evidence at the start of many of the New Testament letters.[12]

Pioneers are met by Jesus

There should also be a link to one of the original apostolic features: exposure to the resurrected living Christ is essential (1 Corinthians 9:1). This first-century phenomenon is, of course, unrepeatable; it is classically defined by meetings with Jesus in the period between the resurrection and the ascension. These meetings are presented to us as historical events, although they stretch the boundaries of our understanding of both presence and physicality. In that Jesus is described as the first fruits of life in the new heaven and new earth, this expansion of horizons is what we might expect. However, encounter with the risen Christ remains possible and essential—but as a spiritual experience. Thus, a pioneer today will be an apostolic person in the sense of being theologically orthodox, including having a spiritual experience of encounter with the risen Jesus and having convictions about the supernatural power of the same risen Christ to change individuals and begin to transform communities.

Pioneers are with the outsiders

There are other implications that stem from the pioneering instinct to go to the edge of what is, where others have not gone before, to work 'where Christ has [not] already been named' (Romans 15:20, RSV). There will be a preference for work with the unchurched, which might equally mean engaging with a particular area or a culture, rather than for work with the lapsed or dechurched. In fairness, some dechurched people could be ex-nominal believers who never truly had a living faith in the first place, and these people do represent a more legitimate apostolic challenge. The presence or absence of life-changing encounter with Jesus is more diagnostic than past ecclesial attendance. Studies of entrepreneurs also suggest that they are naturally good networkers,[13] and studies using the Myers Briggs Personality Indicator always show them as having extravert preferences, deriving energy from being with people rather than alone.[14]

Pioneers are at home with signs

Pioneers will also have some propensity to operate with what are called 'signs of the kingdom', 'power evangelism' or 'signs and wonders' (Romans 15:19, RSV). This has become a contested topic in itself since the ministry in England of John Wimber, nearly 30 years ago, but it has its deeper roots in the signs endemic to Jesus' kingdom ministry and the repeated, almost paralleled, record of the ministries of Peter and Paul in the book of Acts. I add here my understanding that such charismatic gifts were always intended more as signs of mission than for the solace of the saints; nor are they the sole province of charismatics. Of course, with powerful signs come the associated dangers of pride, misuse and misunderstanding, but all these dangers were also encountered by Christ himself and do not negate the presence of this strand within the New Testament. Moreover, in my view, the dispensationalist argument does not stand up biblically; nor does it make any sense of the repeated contemporary worldwide accounts of 'signs' accompanying Christian mission.

Pioneers are flexible to make a difference

Pioneers also seem to be flexible strategists. It has been argued that Paul used a strategy based first upon centres of population, but, within that, adopting a sub-strategy of speaking to Jews first, then to Greeks (Acts 13:46). My suggested modification of this view is that he went wherever people gathered who were 'open'—for example, the riverside in Philippi (Acts 16:13), or both the synagogue and the marketplace/agora in Athens (17:17). Either way, pioneers seek out people in an intentional way.

Once more, there are intriguing connections between the dynamics presented in the apostolic features surrounding Jesus and his apostles and some central observations about entrepreneurs. Bolton and Thompson argue that their creativity and innovation work in the following way. Entrepreneurs, first of all, possess 'a motivation to make a difference'.[15] It is not difficult to map this characteristic on to both Jesus and Paul. It is about more than just their sense of being sent; it includes compassion for those to whom they are sent, and utter conviction that the resultant encounter with God will be both life-giving and life-changing. Next, this motivation has two characteristics that turn intention into practice: entrepreneurs both spot and exploit opportunities. I am nervous of Bolton's word 'exploit' and am glad that it is used as a synonym for 'things are made to happen'.[16] However, the same intentionality is true if the analogy of Jesus' followers as 'fishers of men' has anything to teach us. I have never met a desultory fly fisherman. They can be puzzled, discouraged or frustrated, but they don't go fishing to sit around or do a bit of bird-watching. Fly fishermen watch the water to see where the trout are rising, they compare notes about what flies the fish are taking, and they cast accordingly. Spotting opportunity and taking action is one way of describing this process.

It may be that, willingly or perhaps intuitively, pioneers follow a pattern of concentration and dispersal. Bob Hopkins has argued for many years that this pattern is repeated three times in Acts, emanating from the churches of Jerusalem, Antioch and Ephesus respectively.[17] It seems that God builds up a church as the necessary prelude to disturbing part of that same church, by calling some of its members out to start the process again elsewhere. Hopkins does not use the word 'pioneer' for those who are called onward and outward, but could do so. I conclude that pioneers do not stay long-term to build a big church that operates by in-drag. The length of stay practised by Paul on his journeys in Acts varied from a matter of weeks to several years, and it looks as though his longer stays were at the centres of concentration.

Again I see links to the research about entrepreneurs, which confirms the guesses we have already made. It is characteristic that 'entrepreneurs disturb the status quo. They make a difference because they are different from most of us. They initiate change and enjoy it.'[18]

Pioneers are disturbers of the peace?

I would suggest that we see profound inevitable disturbance caused by the overall ministry of Christ, in the changes to the inherited understanding of Judaism that he both described and embodied. We see disturbance in the unpredicted ministries of Philip to Samaria, in the novel actions of the Cypriot Christians who first evangelised other Greeks at Antioch, and in the creation of uncircumcised Christian communities, with non-observant diets, started by Paul. All of these ministries were as disturbing as they were essential. Thus, we have to note that pioneers may not be easy or comfortable people for others to deal with. At times this was true of Jesus, and of Paul and Peter, though only in Jesus' case can we be confident that he was faultless in the matter.

This characteristic of pioneers does not sit easily with those traditional denominations that, apocryphally, have an eleventh commandment: 'Thou shalt not offend.' They have an attendant disinclination for, and marginalisation of, 'boat rockers'; for, to be English, niceness is an unspoken prerequisite. Yet, to disturb the peace looks like a quality with some biblical roots, connected to those who are first to see what God may be doing that is not containable within the existing arrangements. This is one of many connections to the role of prophecy, which I explore later.

Pioneers are bicultural

A deeper flexibility than simple willingness for geographical deployment marks out a pioneer's engagement with culture. I consider it significant and diagnostic that both Barnabas and Paul had bicultural backgrounds. Is it too daring to map this characteristic also on to the unique dual identity of Jesus of Nazareth, as God the Son and son of Mary? This priceless bicultural gift tends to prevent people from being trapped, in the way that can happen to those who remain living within the only culture they have ever known. It then emanates in a whole variety of responses. From the book of Acts, it looks as though Jewish terms like 'kingdom of God', 'Son of Man' and 'Messiah' were not used in evangelistic contact with secular Greeks, but were confined to those already attending synagogues. Luke is faithfully recording a living process, without reflecting upon it, of what we would now call 'inculturation' and 'double listening'.[19] The process is made explicit in 1 Corinthians 9:19–23, with its summary line, 'I have become all things to all men.'

Pioneers are translators and more

The question is disputed as to whether there is a real and identifiable foundational content to the Christian faith, beneath its initial Jewish clothing. One focus of the debate is about whether or not the Athens mission was a failure, and whether Paul later changed his mind about the content of the message he delivered there (which is the way some people interpret the opening verses of 1 Corinthians 2). It seems to me that the history of mission teaches us that the reality and meaning of the whole historical Jesus event has to be proclaimed afresh not only in each generation but, especially, in each new cultural epoch. One author tracking this approach is Andrew Walls. In Chapter 2 of *The Missionary Movement in Christian History*, he cites six major epochs and, in Chapter 3, describes the need for translation in each case.[20] If Paul is the cross-cultural prototype for this process, then pioneers should be first among those who see the need to carry the good news but to translate it afresh for others. I think Walls is right to think that there is a deeper basis than the need for cultural translation: 'The bewildering paradox at the heart of the Christian confession is not just the obvious one of the divine humanity; it is the twofold affirmation of the utter Jewishness of Jesus and of the boundless universality of the Divine Son.'[21]

This, to me, moves the discussion beyond mere translation of words. In Jesus of Nazareth there is an embodiment of the paradox. As a group, his followers are extremely honoured to be called the body of Christ. Thus, our life too needs to embody this extraordinary mixture of signs of both the eternal and of cultural particularity. Pioneers are significant in that they are the spearhead by which this continued process occurs in the next generation or context. They will be happy to create fresh expressions of church to fit a specific culture—taking as their precedent the differences between first-century Jewish and Greek churches.

However, history teaches us that such changes are not easily accepted and are felt to be disturbing. To try to distinguish what is gospel from what is church, apart from the cultural clothes they are already wearing, is not easy. Yet this is a mission-shaped strand intrinsic to the New Testament. Two classic cases, in the early church, were about who the believers might eat with and whether or not circumcision was necessary. We can see with hindsight that while Paul gets it, Peter struggles; with Cornelius, in Acts 10, Peter makes the necessary leap, but, in the events described in Galatians 2, he relapses as tradition overmasters fresh discovery.

Pioneers are developers

From the New Testament and the strands linked to being apostolic, I see the following abilities as key for pioneers. I am agnostic over whether pioneer-starters have this cluster of abilities in its entirety. However, pioneer-sustainers are far more likely to have them all, and so they may be a closer gift-set match to the entrepreneur.

Pioneers are able to teach and to respond to problems in the local church. Paul clearly thought he should pass on what had been passed in the first place to him (1 Corinthians 4:17; 11:23), and many of the epistles were written as a teaching response to the young churches' needs and difficulties. A vital consequence of one of the pioneer's primary characteristics, that of leaving, is that pioneers are also able and willing to hand on the work by appointing presbyteral leaders to take the work forward (Acts 14:23; Titus 1:5).[22] Later missiology has taught us that this should not be a once-for-all step, but that the matter is one of making disciple-making-disciples and leaders who will raise up leaders to continue the self-reproducing nature of the church, which is itself perennially apostolic.

Pioneers will be able to have this ripple effect only if they can relate, love and encourage.[23] By personal example, they work with the grace of God to raise up the next generation. The emphasis in the Gospels on the love of Christ for his disciples, and, in the letters of John, Peter and Paul, the attitudes exhibited by the authors to their recipients, would be my ground for this assertion. Here, I think, there is a particular challenge to goal-orientated initiators. Sadly, I have come across examples in which there are echoes of attitudes more characteristic of exploitative employers or uncaring generals.

The last ability I want to list here is the ability to accept suffering. I began this chapter by exploring the links between the titles given to Jesus in Hebrews and Acts. The same text that describes him as the 'pioneer and perfecter of our faith' says that he is the one 'who for the joy that was set before him endured the cross, despising the shame...' (Hebrews 12:2). If this was Jesus' pattern and we are followers of this pioneer, daring to be named as his body, we cannot avoid this connection. In 1 Peter, it is very clear that joining in the sufferings of Christ is the pathway to glory. Paul, in 2 Corinthians 4, sees a death-leading-to-life pattern, itself an echo of Christ's teaching in John 12. If pioneers are seed-sowers, it will be so for them too.

Pioneers are prophetic

I link many of these strands to the role of the prophet, because those with this gifting also pioneer, in that they see what has not been seen previously. As such, prophetic people are rather different from entrepreneurs. They are seers, not doers. But why make this link? Partly, it takes seriously the comment that the Church is built upon the foundation (another image that connects to being first, or at the beginning) of the apostles and prophets (Ephesians 2:20; 3:5). This is not true just historically, but also dynamically. So we might read Ephesians 4 and remark that unless people are sent (apostolic) and they hear God (prophetic), they will have nothing appropriate to say (evangelistic: how can they preach unless they are sent? Romans 10:15); then, as a result, there is no one to pastor or teach. There is also the connection that sometimes the prophetic embodies or acts out the message. As such, pioneers act out the fact that mission is always at the edge of what is; they embody the translation and inculturation task of the church; they personify the temporary, tabernacle-like characteristic that is inherent in being church and that Christendom influences have largely obscured.

We see the prophetic at work among the New Testament pioneers, firstly noting Jesus in John's Gospel, who 'sees' what the Father is doing (5:19). We meet it in the Spirit's redirection of Paul and Barnabas, telling them to go to Macedonia rather than Bithynia. It is revealed in the time taken to listen to God by Jesus at prayer, by Paul during his years in the desert, and by Peter on the rooftop at Joppa. We observe the prophetic courage that enables the apostles to stand against the tide of public opinion in Acts.

We should also note the need to be humble enough to acknowledge that prophetic insights are partial (1 Corinthians 13:12) and not all is revealed (Acts 20:22). We should discipline ourselves to use the gift to strengthen, comfort and encourage (1 Corinthians 14:3) and for the common good (12:7). In these ways, and with these bits of advice, the prophetic is also a pioneering feature. Apostolic pioneers do well to attend to prophetic dimensions, without being lured into unaccountable and unchallengeable certitude.

Practical implications

As I have said, I always suspected that the training and deployment of our recent pioneers would present the greatest challenges. Here I highlight but three of the dangers to be avoided.

The wrong diet

One danger is that traditional training and recognition have, both socially and academically, domesticated the foundational pioneering missional roles and even denied them validity. Today I hear, quite widely, that the experience of pioneers at theological colleges and courses is akin to that of carnivores being fed a herbivore diet, with the odd soya burger thrown in. In my view, we have merely added some content to the existing diet designed for pastor/teachers and priests. We seem unable to recognise that pioneers are different. However, being rare is different from being odd or deluded.[24] Freely allowing pioneers (whether lay or ordained) to train through very different, mission-centred, more apprentice-based processes, as used by CMS or Church Army, would be a great step forward.

I am concerned, too, that courses like MSM, though valuable in firing the imagination and equipping the minds of congregational members, do not address the problems of energised laity who are trying to innovate in the face of resistant local clergy. In my experience, the latter hold the whip hand, stifling initiatives or bringing them to nothing.

Mismatch

I am also unconvinced by the current ordained pioneer-curacy patterns. We are meeting problems of supervision, in that their incumbents often don't understand them. They are also being unduly loaded with training for traditional roles: it isn't that diffi-cult to learn how to take a funeral! They are being distracted with significant responsibilities and commitments to lead traditional congregations. We are not making due allowance for previous life experience, and so we are not setting at least some of them free early enough. Thus, we have a strategic disconnection between two things. There is an acknowledged need to plant churches in large areas of new housing, for which 14 dioceses have made successful large bids for money to the Church Commissioners. However, we are finding it difficult to find appropriate leaders for these opportunities, at the very same time as pioneers are stuck in the kind of curacies that don't really give them the scope they need.

What happens if you succeed?

A pioneer worth her or his salt, given deployment to a context where a local church has made a start in being missionary, should, with a fair wind, have a fresh expression of church started and heading towards being viable within the first three to four years, but no one seems to have thought out what happens next. We are not asking the question, 'How will such a venture escape the marginalisation long associated with erstwhile daughter congregations,[25] or the rollercoaster ride linked for decades with youth groups?' We will have learnt nothing if the pioneers simply come to the end of their training period and are sent elsewhere. The very focus on their training is preventing a focus on the life of a young fresh expression. In the historic denominations, it is sadly typical to think first of the ministerial issues and fail to think through what is going on for a young Christian community.

Moreover, pioneers are not rare bizarre ministers (whether lay or ordained) wearing L plates, who should be assimilated into the system. They are there to listen and see, to initiate, to disturb, and to be taken seriously as they create what was not. Thus, the new Christian communities that they bring to birth will, in turn, flourish, engage with post-Christendom society, find their own identity within the wider family of local churches and, under God, become part of the leaven that renews the whole lump of the Church. In practice, we have no vision of this disturbing sodality;[26] we are not awake to the rising up of a fresh set of friars in our midst, and we are not yet really serious about the fact that they are what it says on the tin—pioneers.

Notes

1 G. Cray (ed), *Mission-Shaped Church* (CHP, 2004), p. 147. The text reads, 'The Ministry Division of the Archbishops' Council should actively seek to encourage the identification, selection and training of pioneer church planters, for both lay and ordained ministries, through its appropriate channels to bishops' selectors, diocesan Reader Boards and training institutions. Specific selection criteria should be established. Patterns of training should reflect the skills, gifting and experiences of those being trained.'

2 In using the term 'pioneer', I do not mean the adjective that could qualify many spheres of work, but a shorthand for the recent designation 'Lay and Ordained Pioneer Minsters'.

3 G. Abbott-Smith, *Manual Greek Lexicon of the New Testament* (T&T Clark, 1968), p. 62.

4 It would be onerous to list all the Johannine references. Suffice it to say that the sent identity of Jesus occurs six times in John 5 and five times in John 6, while his sending of us is encapsulated by John 20:21.

5 See also J. Lawrence, *Growing Leaders* (BRF, 2004), pp. 195–213, on the leader and vision.

6 B. Bolton & J. Thompson, *Entrepreneurs* (Butterworth-Heinemann, 2000), p. 5.

7 Bolton & Thompson, *Entrepreneurs*, p. 22.

8 Eddie Gibbs, *Followed or Pushed?* (MARC, 1987). 'There can be no leaders without followers' (p. 151).

9 C.K. Barrett, *The Signs of an Apostle* (Paternoster, 1996), p. 86.

10 V. Donovan, *Christianity Rediscovered* (SCM, 1982), p. 163.

11 I know that in the early centuries the issues of apostolic faithfulness and apostolic succession were held to be more important, and rivalry between them continues. Yet the scholar Barrett, reading the New Testament, is content to describe them as 'wandering missionaries' who 'found Christian societies' (*Signs of an Apostle*, p. 91).

12 See Barrett, *Signs of an Apostle*, pp. 12–13, arguing that being sent by Christ was foundational.

13 Bolton & Thompson, *Entrepreneurs*, p. 24.

14 Bolton & Thompson, *Entrepreneurs*, p. 17.

15 Bolton & Thompson, *Entrepreneurs*, p. 27.

16 Bolton & Thompson, *Entrepreneurs*, p. 28.

17 This argument first appeared in a partial version in the 1988 Grove Evangelism booklet No 4, B. Hopkins, *Church Planting: Models for Mission*, pp. 11–12. It is developed in B. Hopkins & R. White, *Enabling Church Planting* (CPAS, 1995), p. 5. A short version occurs within Hopkins, 'Institutional and local change through church plants', in M. Mills-Powell (ed.), *Setting the Church of England Free* (John Hunt Publishing, 2003), pp. 139–140.

18 Bolton & Thompson, *Entrepreneurs*, p. 22.

19 Both are explored in *Mission-Shaped Church*: the first in pp. 105–116 and the second in pp. 104–105.

20 A. Walls, *The Missionary Movement in Christian History* (T&T Clark, 1996).

21 Walls, *Missionary Movement in Christian History*, p. xvi.

22 See also Gibbs, *Followed or Pushed?* p. 12.

23 See Gibbs, *Followed or Pushed?* pp. 151–159. Also see Lawrence, *Growing Leaders*, pp. 175–190, and on leaders embodying values and enabling community, pp. 237–247.

24 Bolton & Thompson review studies on how common entrepreneurship is, and offer an uncertain spectrum from 1 per cent to 10–15 per cent of the population (*Entrepreneurs*, pp. 3–4).

25 A term used for the starting of new congregations, structurally dependent on the parish church, in the 1930s and 1950s.

26 See via the Internet, Ralph Winter, *The Two Structures of God's Redemptive Mission*, an address given to the All-Asia Mission Consultation in Seoul, Korea, in August 1973.

3

The gift of troublesome questioning: pioneers and learning

Beth Keith

Twenty years ago, Steve and Anne were leading a youth programme in a suburban church, which was growing numerically and seeing a number of young people come to faith and grow as Christians. They then moved to an inner-city area and began by trying to recreate the activities that had previously worked well, but none of them seemed to work in the new context. At this point, they stepped back and began to reflect on what they had done before and why they had done it, and also on the new culture in which they found themselves. This helped them to see how much of their previous work had been dependent on the context, and the experience caused them to question the assumptions behind their practice. Over time they developed new practices that worked in their current context, which led to the planting of a church in a very different style. Since then, Steve has developed contextual mission further, now working with pagans and new agers, regularly doing ministry at mind/body/spirit fairs.

Steve's journey is perhaps a common one, shared by others who have found their ecclesiology changing as they have engaged with a new mission context. Through this process, Steve and others have developed some of the new forms of church that we see emerging in the UK today. However, alongside this, there are many examples of initiatives labelled as fresh expressions of church, which do not live up to the name. They may be good examples of mission or ministry from existing churches but they are not new churches growing out of contextual mission and engaging with people outside the church. By looking at the cognitive processes involved in this process of contextual mission, I want to show why some individuals manage to develop wildly creative, yet orthodox, forms of church, and why it still remains relatively uncommon. We will see how a deep engagement with the context occurs, allowing the new experiences of that context to shape understanding and question existing ecclesiological practices and assumptions. While being a transformative skill, it is perhaps the element of questioning existing practice and assumptions that makes this gift both troublesome and uncommon within the church. In understanding more of how the process works, we will be better placed to identify and support this gift within the mixed economy of church life.

Adapters and stabilisers

We learn by engaging with and experiencing our context, accumulating existing meanings and adapting them to new and perhaps contradictory experiences. When we are babies, our minds are formed by interaction with our environment. Each new experience both develops cognitive networks and interacts with existing ones. New information is assimilated into the existing neural network and adapted to fit with existing data. Alongside this, new information can cause an accommodation or change in the existing data, balancing inconsistencies between existing 'knowns' and contradictory new experiences.[1] As we experience more things, our understanding develops through this assembling and reordering of the mind, which becomes an immense yet flexible network of ideas, thoughts and feelings. As old and new data are weighed and balanced for inconsistencies,[2] new understandings affect our thoughts and actions, causing change. This is a hugely complex process, and, while the image of assembling and reordering is a simplistic representation, it does help to build a picture of how we interact with new experiences. The balancing of old and new occurs with any new experience, although the process is heightened in times of social change, when new experiences are more frequent.

By adulthood, individuals have developed this complex balancing process between new information and existing knowledge. However, some individuals will interact more readily with new and contradictory experiences, willingly altering existing data to correspond with new information. I call these people 'adapters'. With a predominant tendency to reorder, adapters have a fluid and responsive relationship to their environment. They are able to negotiate and adapt to new experiences and so engage in transformative change. This tendency is evident in some pioneers' ability to adapt old religious data to new cultural data in a coherent manner.

Conversely, others will find it challenging to interact with new experiences, often rejecting the new information in order to maintain their existing knowledge. I call these people 'stabilisers'. A predominant tendency towards stabilising will mean that they adapt new experiences to fit into existing data. This enables a stability of meanings and understanding and so leads to slow, progressive modification—or, in extreme cases, inertia.

Both stabilisers and adapters have positive and negative attributes, depending on context. In a fluid context where rapid change is required, an adapter will feel more at ease and will thrive in the environment. In the same context, a stabiliser is likely to feel threatened and overwhelmed by the extent of the new experiences being encountered and so will withdraw, reducing the amount of their exposure to new information. However, in a relatively stable situation or a context requiring slow adaptation over long periods of time, a stabiliser will act intuitively at an appropriate pace of development. In this context, an adapter may get frustrated at the slow pace of change and so modify programmes or activities in an attempt to kick-start change. This allows them to use their adaptation skills, but their action will be based on their own drive to reorder rather than on an appropriate response to context.

Interestingly, given the same experience and context, adapters and stabilisers will not only act differently but will actually process the experience differently.

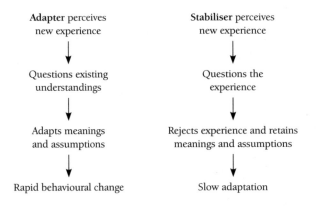

Adapter perceives new experience

↓

Questions existing understandings

↓

Adapts meanings and assumptions

↓

Rapid behavioural change

Stabiliser perceives new experience

↓

Questions the experience

↓

Rejects experience and retains meanings and assumptions

↓

Slow adaptation

Transformative critique

Adapters are able to respond more quickly to cultural change because the new experiences they encounter readily create changes in meanings and assumptions. This enables rapid and sometimes unstable change. Key to this process is the ability to engage in critical reflection on existing understandings. It is this level of critique, willingly reordering and even rejecting previous understandings, that enables the transformation of thoughts, behaviour and practices. Conversely, where assumptions are taken for granted, outcomes are necessarily limited by the nature of those assumptions.

For example, let's take a possible Anglican assumption [A] that although the primary unit of church is a diocese, this is best delivered—or, perhaps, even necessarily delivered—locally through the parish structure. How do stabilisers and adapters respond differently to the experience of decline in church attendance? Let's take the stabiliser's response first (see figure 1).

Figure 1: A stabiliser's response to decline in church attendance

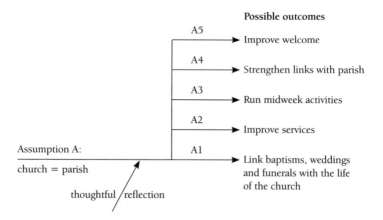

A stabiliser encountering a drop in church attendance may perceive it as stemming from the church's failure to connect with the parish. Accepting assumption A, that church is best delivered within the parish structure, a stabiliser is likely to engage in thoughtful reflection over how the parish could be improved, leading to a number of options (A1, A2, A3 and so on). This process of thoughtful reflection will enable some slow, progressive adaptation between the parish church and the wider community. However, in contexts where transformational change is required, as recommended in the *Mission-Shaped Church* report (pp. 1–15), this type of thoughtful reflection may yield outcomes that are too limited in scope.

Given the same experience, an adapter will tend towards more critical reflection, questioning the necessity and appropriateness of assumption A, that church is best delivered as parish. This type of critical reflection dramatically increases the number of possible outcomes by enabling existing knowledge and underlying assumptions to be questioned (see figure 2).

Figure 2: An adapter's response to decline in church attendance

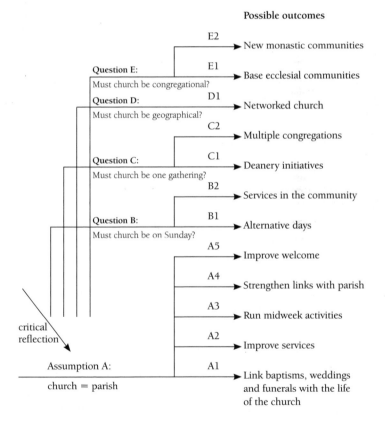

Possible outcomes

E2 → New monastic communities

Question E:
Must church be congregational?

E1 → Base ecclesial communities

Question D:
Must church be geographical?

D1 → Networked church

C2 → Multiple congregations

Question C:
Must church be one gathering?

C1 → Deanery initiatives

B2 → Services in the community

Question B:
Must church be on Sunday?

B1 → Alternative days

A5 → Improve welcome

A4 → Strengthen links with parish

A3 → Run midweek activities

critical
reflection

A2 → Improve services

Assumption A:
church = parish

A1 → Link baptisms, weddings and funerals with the life of the church

Reflection that incorporates this level of critique opens up many more possible outcomes by allowing the individual to reject the initial assumption A. In a relatively short number of reflective moves, numerous outcomes, independent of assumption A, can develop. This progression readily transforms belief, behaviour and practice, allowing the individual to move further beyond the original assumptions. So we see in this example that critical reflection on parish-based assumptions very quickly yields multiple options, some moving a considerable distance from parish structures, such as networked church, new monastic communities or base ecclesial communities.

Structural assumptions such as 'church must be parish' can be readily identified and critiqued, although they are hard to change as this may involve systemic change. Assumptions that are socially rather than structurally organised can be more readily adapted but can be more difficult to identify.

In a recent discussion I had with a pioneer, Chris, he talked about his frustration in developing discipleship within the fresh expressions of church that he was leading. As the conversation progressed, it became clear that the difficulty was about developing relational discipleship, which bore similarities with the mode of discipleship he had experienced himself as a young Christian. As we talked, he was able to reflect critically on whether his assumption about relational discipleship was appropriate. He then started to imagine other possible ways to develop discipleship, which fitted better with the context and existing behaviour of the group. In this case, a subtle change of practice, while holding on to the principle of discipleship, may well produce wide-ranging changes within the life of a new Christian community.

This type of transformative change occurs internally within an individual and is then worked out through external changes to behaviour and practice. This process of internal transformation, beginning with the pioneer and leading to change in Christian communities, is seen clearly in autobiographical stories of cross-cultural mission, such as Vincent Donovan's account of his mission with the Masai. As he experienced life alongside the Masai, these new experiences called into question some of the assumptions of his existing religious beliefs and practices:

At that moment, facing me was that vast, sprawling, all-pervasive complex of customs and traditions and values and dictates of human behaviour which was Masai culture, a nation in the biblical sense, to which I had to bring the gospel. At this point I had to make the humiliating admission that I did not know what the gospel was. During those days I spent long hours thinking long, difficult thoughts, and sometimes frightening ones, about the momentous task that faced me— the bringing together of a culture and the gospel…

… starting with a clear mind, a mind free of preconceptions, [as] there is no other way to deal with a subject that is so strange to us. If we allow our minds and our attitudes to be filled with the convictions and conclusions arising from our pastoral experience, I think we will never arrive at the freedom necessary to make first evangelisation possible and understandable.[3]

The process of unlearning belief and practice in a new context is as important to the pioneer as simply learning more about the new context. Another pioneer leader, Liz, explained that as she engaged with the needs of the community, she was led to her own questions about how the church could respond to those needs. She was not trying to be creative or start something new, but the context forced her to ask hard questions about whether the church, in its current practice, could help and support the young people with whom she was working. Through this level of critique, she was able to imagine and then develop church in new ways.

Is all adaptation good?

So far, I have taken a neutral stance in looking at how we adapt to or stabilise our exposure to new experiences from a cognitive perspective. This neutral stance is entirely appropriate within a scientific context, where adaptation to an evolving environment carries its own merit and validity. However, within the Christian context, in which other elements pertaining to orthodoxy provide validity, it is not the case that all adaptation is good. The landscape has changed remarkably within the last 20 years, with contextual mission moving from the domain of overseas mission and entering into the psyche of the church in the UK. This marks a swing away from closely defined liberal, evangelical or catholic theologies and churchmanship, and towards something unknown and developmental, with an emphasis on mission, diversity, dialogue and evolving belief and practice. At worst, the latter could be described as an unconsidered, syncretistic pick-and-mix. At best, however, we can see new ecclesial communities emerging out of a variety of contexts from which the church had become disconnected. This reconnection, blending innovation and orthodoxy, is driven by the Spirit in mission, moving towards an exploratory connection with historic and global faith traditions through a serious engagement with context.

Unsurprisingly, such exploration creates a reasonably high level of uncertainty within the church. However, while it may feel like a time of risky experimentation, it is worth remembering that this is not a new experience. Within scripture and within the life of the Church, we see the repeated emergence of new forms of belief and practice in connection with cultural adaptation. During the Babylonian exile, as well as during the development of the early Church, religious practice and belief were adapted as the people of God engaged with their context (see Jeremiah 29:1–7; Acts 15:1–35). This dialectic narrative between ecclesial communities and their context is in evidence across the broad sweeping paradigms of the Church, as epochs of Christianity have mirrored epochs of culture.[4] The rise and decline of the main historical expressions of the Church parallel cultural movements globally as new forms of faith grow alongside cultural developments.[5] The dialectic narrative between gospel and culture is also seen clearly in the emergence of sodal movements such as monastic movements and missionary societies.[6]

This repeating pattern of contextualisation is often associated with the emergence of new practices, which in turn recreate and rejuvenate the Church in times of decline.[7] However, the pattern is also associated with opposition, misunderstanding and conflict within the church.[8]

While critical reflection enables transformation, this level of change remains uncommon. Pioneers often express the constraints or opposition they experience as they engage in questioning church assumptions. Common themes currently emerging from conversations with pioneers include the ways in which they are shrinking the scope of their vision and practice to within acceptable modes of ministry, reducing critical reflection when it is viewed as threatening. Romano, in his account of the founders of monastic orders within the Roman Catholic Church, notes that one of the marks of a pioneer is their ability to question aspects of church without drawing the church into question.[9] However, the difference between questioning an aspect of the church and the church calling into question is subtle, especially given the role of the institutional church in authorising pioneer ministry and the often complex tension between institution and pioneer. The words of critique, whether expressed by the pioneer as an individual or embodied in the alternative practices of a new ecclesial community, may question an aspect of the church that is held, at the time, as essential to the existence of the church. Therefore, to question that particular aspect is understood—by some, though not others—as drawing into question the church itself. Romano describes this as the 'institutional confusion' often present within the institutional church, as a response to pioneers. This common institutional response exhibits stabiliser tendencies and the inability to adapt old data in the light of new experiences. The lack of permission to engage in transformative critique may hinder pioneers' abilities to imagine new possibilities.

Constraints to adaptive ability

In the course of my work, I have carried out a critical reflection exercise on the essential and beneficial elements of church with just over 100 pioneers.[10] While observing this exercise, I noticed a clear correlation between ordained ministry and nervousness about questioning church practices. Non-ordained pioneers were, in general, better able to discuss differences between essential and beneficial elements of church. Participants who were ordained or in ordination training tended to struggle with this, and exhibited anxiety in evaluating the differences between essential and beneficial elements. They argued for a much higher retention of certain church practices as being 'essential' than other participants did—for example, a church name, a building, or a Sunday service.

This is a complex issue and is influenced by a variety of factors. Were these pioneers selected as 'safe' because they were less likely to question existing church assumptions? Did the formation process encourage their 'safe' approach or did the pressure of their jobs have an impact on the exercise? It is not clear what led to their anxiety over critical reflection, but the findings do seem to confirm other research carried out across a variety of institutions, showing how difficult it is to implement critical reflection—even where critical reflection terminology is applied—as pressures within institutions tend to encourage the unquestioning acceptance of underlying assumptions.[11]

Encouraging critical reflection on the essential and contextual elements of church is not to suggest that all church practice is contextual, without any essential elements or identifiable marks. Nor is it to suggest that anything can be 'church', or that practices and beliefs can be readily and unquestioningly thrown aside in the name of mission. However, the difference in levels of anxiety and defensiveness caused simply by asking this type of question is a concern. Surely anyone ministering today must develop the ability to discern how elements of church can grow appropriately in the given context, and, for this to happen, permission to question existing practice is necessary. There are a number of tools available to enable a critical reflection on church practice—for example, the Marks of the Church, Seven Sacred Spaces, and the Fresh Expressions journey.[12]

The ability to engage in transformative critique is the ability to question well, to have the tools to sift between contextual and enduring elements of church. It requires pioneers to have enough confidence in understanding church to be able to adapt practices and expressions of belief. The ability to question assumptions enables pioneers to move beyond existing practices, and yet this process is vulnerable to social and systemic pressures. The ability comes through the practice of questioning assumptions, by which practitioners gain confidence in their ability to hold lightly to existing cultural practices, while exploring new ways in which the body of Christ is becoming expressed.

Moving forward together

Day-to-day, pioneers are encountering the classic tension between adapters and stabilisers, as they and other adapters in the local church seek to question and modify existing practices in the light of the context, whilst stabilisers seek to engage further with the context by reinforcing assumptions and existing practices. There is inevitable conflict and misunderstanding, but our commitment to the body of Christ, and our understanding of Jesus, require a different response:

We walk past each other and in each other's absence; and even when we speak face to face, it is often in a 'lock' of mutual suspicion and deep anxiety. But the Body of Christ requires more than this. It requires… staying alongside… to say to one another, from time to time, hopefully and gently, 'Do you see that? This is how I see him: can you see him too?' [13]

In my recent Master's dissertation study, 27 pioneers from different areas of England were asked to share briefly about their ministry, highlighting a challenge and an encouragement. Of those working within parishes, 67 per cent noted their primary difficulty as being the development of new practices alongside established congregations. The issues discussed ranged from opposition to new practices to difficulties in balancing the dual roles of mission and parish ministry, where existing practice was often taken to be the priority and new practices were misunderstood. In stark contrast, all five participants who were working in ministry roles outside parish structures identified key challenges that related to their mission context. Many of those who are pioneering from traditional structures expect to spend time negotiating and educating the existing church community about mission. However, that this might become their primary challenge is often a surprise to them. Excessive time spent on validating the process of contextualisation and reimagining church shifts the focus from the mission context to the existing church community. One pioneer had even moved from parish oversight and towards mission agency oversight, due to the tensions between established churchmanship and the emerging ministry. If fresh expressions of church are to be planted from traditional forms of church, such as parish or deanery structures, as well as through movements such as new monastic orders or mission agencies, more understanding between established church practices and emerging missional communities will be crucial.

It is time to remember that the ability to ask troublesome questions is not a threat but a gift for the church. The Northumbria Community express it as one of their values, provocatively calling it 'the heretical imperative'.[14] It is time to be open to difference and to learn from one another. Becoming more aware of our own perspective and intuitive response to new experiences, whether that is a tendency to adapt or a tendency to stabilise, will enable us to step back from our initial response, reflect, and communicate perceptions in a less threatening or defensive way.

Hearing the experiences of other pioneers and stories from a range of fresh expressions of church helps to ground a local exploration in the wider movement within the church, both validating and releasing the imagination. Sharetheguide.org is a great resource for this purpose, drawing together a breadth of experience and reflection on fresh expressions of church. Building relationships with other pioneers and permission-givers offers places to dialogue and critique which are both supportive and challenging. Agencies such as Church Army and CMS, with their unique role, have much to offer the wider church, being closely related to church structures but having years of wisdom and experience in developing new forms of mission and evangelism. Finding ways to communicate both the process of contextual mission and the resulting ecclesiology, which reduce misunderstanding, will be essential for the further development of contextual mission. This will require movement and collaboration both from pioneers of the new and from guardians of the established order.

The best pioneers imaginatively live out and create expressions of church that differ greatly from the practices they inherited. The ability to develop contextual, yet orthodox, expressions of faith requires a creative engagement with new experiences, in partnership with the Spirit in mission, to work with fidelity to Christ. Through this process, fresh expressions of church are being developed that bring something wildly new—signs of the Spirit at work in renewing and recreating the church. If the church selects and authorises only 'safe' pioneers who will not question church assumptions, yet asks them to develop new forms of church, it is asking for the impossible. Where questions cannot be asked,

61

ecclesial assumptions will act as earplugs, hampering pioneers as they try to listen to both the context and the Spirit at work. Together we can create an environment within the church that recognises the ability to ask troublesome questions as a gift. Together we can choose not to be threatened by transformative critique. We can walk alongside and yet graciously challenge and support pioneers as they go further. Then they will be more creative and will carry into their contexts the treasures of the church, as we all follow Christ.

Notes

1　Jennifer A. Moon, *A Handbook of Reflective and Experiential Learning, Theory & Practice* (Routledge Falmer, 2004), pp. 16–17; J. Piaget, *Biology and Knowledge* (Edinburgh University Press, 1971); H. Gleitman, *Psychology* (W.W. Norton, 1992), p. 507.

2　D. Boud et al., *Reflection: Turning experience into learning* (Routledge Falmer, 1985), pp. 31–35.

3　Vincent Donovan, *Christianity Rediscovered* (SCM, 2001), pp. 25–26.

4　Hans Küng, *Christianity: The religious situation of our time* (SCM, 1995), pp. 938–939.

5　David J. Bosch, *Transforming Mission: Paradigm shifts in theology of mission* (Orbis, 1991), pp. 181–189.

6　A. Romano, *The Charism of the Founders* (St Pauls, date), p. 135; R.D. Winter, *The Two Structures of God's Redemptive Mission* (All-Asia Mission Consultation, date).

7　A.F. Walls, *The Missionary Movement in Christian History* (Orbis, 1996), p. 145.

8　David Knowles, *The Religious Orders in England* (CUP, date), p. 188; Romano, *The Charism of the Founders*, p. 121.

9　Romano, *The Charism of the Founders*, p. 61.

10　These practitioners participated in the critical reflection at training events run by ReSource, at the Greenbelt festival and at St John's College, Nottingham.

11　Raanan Lipshitz, 'Chic, mystique and misconception: Argyris and Schon and the rhetoric of organizational learning', *The Journal of Applied Behavioural Science* (vol. date), p. 471.

12　*Mission-Shaped Church* (CHP, 2009), p. 96; *Encounter on the Edge* no. 43 (date); www.sharetheguide.org/develop

13　Rowan Williams, *Making Moral Decisions* (CUP, 2000), p. 14.

14　www.northumbriacommunity.org/who-we-are/the-rule-briefly

A pioneer's story

Dave and I (a Methodist Deacon) were sent to St Athan, South Wales, in 2005 to be involved in a new church building project. What developed and emerged was probably not in the minds of the small remnant of five Methodists who made the move a mile up the road to temporary facilities, and subsequently into the new building situated adjacent to the housing estate where we lived. By building relationships and being fully part of the community, we wanted to provide a context in which people could explore the Christian faith in a way that connected with their daily lives and the issues they faced. 'Mosaic' was born—a gathering of people, at first monthly and then (since January 2009) weekly on Sundays. All ages are part of the Mosaic community and we now have a regular gathering of 40–50 people; the majority of them have had little or no prior contact with any church and are from the local ex-RAF estates. Mosaic is creative, participatory and community focused, and has grown alongside our community development work.

Here are some of the issues and challenges we have faced and what we have learned through them.

Isolation

The chasm has been great between our own practice, born out of a particular understanding of mission and being church, and the predominantly elderly and/or traditional congregations within the circuit. We have often felt frustrated and disheartened that people don't share our vision. Sometimes, established ministers and mature Christians have a fixed theology and understanding about church but, if hand was held on heart, they would love to see the life and transformation that we have witnessed in their own contexts.

Interestingly, it is more often the unchurched and those with whom we journeyed and serve who understand something of the spiritual dynamic occurring. Initially we tried hard to inspire others to embrace what God was already doing in their communities, and it was draining. We have often felt apathetic about even trying to keep on explaining and encouraging others to be risk-takers and pioneers. Instead, we have tended to embrace an attitude of simply doing what we sense God has called us to do among those who are hearing the good news of the kingdom of God for the first time.

Personal cost

For us, it has been costly in terms of being available 24/7, sharing our journey with the local community and living it out publicly. We have often found ourselves fatigued, emotionally overwhelmed and hypercritical in evaluation. Some of this is to do with the lack of a supportive local network: the distance between us and our family and friends has been too great to allow regular visits. We appreciate the long phone calls! We have had a regular day off every week, when we have left the estate for some space and external nourishment.

When you have a creative, prophetic or pioneering spirit, it can become painful to carry and give birth to something new. Often, you are trying to give the people around you an accurate description of what you believe God is creating, without fully knowing all the answers, variables and potential. Therefore, until something of the vision is actually born, you can encounter many quizzical faces and unanswerable questions. When birth comes, people need constant encouragement to embrace, encounter and become fully part of the new creation before adopting it and perceiving God at work within it.

In terms of personal growth, it has become a significant part of our journey to take a day a month for personal reflection—to take time out to discern what God is doing, what we have learnt and where we might be being led. Working as a husband-and-wife partnership has been challenging. At times we have been so exhausted that we have had nothing left to give each other. Sometimes we have run with too many ideas.

Ourselves

Our biggest challenge has probably been ourselves. We have been burdened with our own fears, doubts and sense of failure. Initially we agonised over whether Mosaic was 'church' or not, and whether it was of God or just our own idea. The people who seem to understand are fellow pioneers. It has been invaluable to meet with those who speak the same language, for advice, affirmation and reassurance that we are simply OK.

Letting go

We have found it hard to entrust others with what has felt like our 'baby'. We have been reluctant to let people be involved in the leadership for fear of the vision being hijacked and 'churchified'. Pioneers are not often surrounded by like-minded people. It requires large amounts of trust to let go and let others grow into leadership. For us, to have to move on after five years is extremely painful but we have to trust that God is at the heart of what is growing here.

Vulnerability

Learning that God calls us as we are, and that that is who we need to be among people, has been most significant. People need to know we are fully human and share some of the same issues as them, even though we are Christians. It is in this vulnerability that people have openly shared and entrusted themselves to us. It reveals a God who identifies with us.

And now for some high points:

- We have been able to journey with people who have little or no theological background and have had the freedom to explore Christianity from scratch in creative, dynamic and contextual ways. We have been working on a blank canvas with many people who have had no preconceived picture of church.
- We have seen sceptics in our community come to accept that something beautiful has happened among them and that their quality of life has improved.
- We sense that we have been part of something greater than ourselves and, in our weakness, God has used what we have offered.
- We have seen amazing transformation in people's lives. Two teenage boys who left our estate travel the 45-minute journey back every Sunday to continue to be part of Mosaic. Older teenage lads say that they would not normally 'be seen dead in church' but love coming to Mosaic.

What an amazing journey we have been privileged to share with this community! Now it is time to let go and entrust it into God's hands and the hands of our successors. We look forward to hearing how it continues to grow.

Michelle and David Legumi have pioneered a new Christian community in South Wales over the last five years. They are now being sent to Falmouth, Cornwall, to work alongside a large, well-established town centre Methodist Church, to help them engage with the local community.

4

The icebergs of expectation: personal issues pioneers face

David Male

When I was planting the Net Church in Huddersfield, it often felt like being at the top and bottom of a rollercoaster at the same time! There were times of great elation and excitement, and yet, often concurrently, there was also a huge sense of frailty and nervousness about the future. It needs to be said clearly that it is hard being a pioneer at times, but I would not want to change from that calling and I know that most pioneers feel the same way.

Does this mean that being a pioneer is more difficult than any other ministry position in a church? I would certainly not claim that, but I think there are unique issues that the pioneer faces in breaking new ground, starting from scratch and being the first in new situations. It concerns me that many pioneers I meet are very worn down by their pioneering, and some are fast approaching burn-out. We need to ensure that we are learning to pioneer in life-affirming ways, even though pioneering will also often require hardship and sacrifice.

Expectations

The biggest issue that pioneers face is expectations. Expectations are like icebergs. We only see about ten per cent of what is really there, and they can easily bring disaster for us or our fledgling community. It is very important to spend time trying to discern what expectations are in operation around your activities. We need to operate with good expectation management. This is complicated by the fact that expectations come from different sources and can even bring conflicting requirements. We will have our own expectations as we pioneer an initiative, as will our team, our sending church, our denomination and the people with whom we are connecting. Try meeting all those expectations and it's not surprising that you might feel exhausted!

I think the issue is particularly acute when you are starting to develop a new community. It will be very precious and important to you, driven by the God-given vision that you and others have followed. You may have had to make many sacrifices simply to get to the starting line. The very nature of what you are beginning will be risky, with all the emotional reactions that this might provoke in you.

In my experience of pioneering situations, the pressure is often so intense that any weaknesses can be cruelly exposed—involving spiritual, psychical or emotional issues that we have not yet really faced. It is very hard to hide these issues in such an exposed place as a pioneering situation. Pioneering calls for a robust life, in which we are aware of our inevitable weaknesses but also seeking a maturing and developing life that enables and encourages us to be fully human.

The first expectation you may need to manage is associated with hype. It is very easy for you and/or others to feel that your initiative is a return to the glory days of church life and you are the answer to all the church's problems and ills! People may want to hype the story of your new, creative church community, which puts greater pressure on you to succeed. I started something very small recently in Cambridge and immediately I had numerous requests for media coverage of what we were trying to do. My strong advice would be to resist advertising yourselves and your achievements at first. Get on with what God is calling you to do and leave the PR to him. You need to keep the expectations realistic in the early days, for your own sake, and so that you don't allow outside pressures and interest to deflect you from your God-given task.

Linked to this is the problem of measuring 'success'—whatever we mean by that word in our own context. We all need to feel that we have done a good job or achieved what we set out to do. But what does 'success' for your fresh expression actually look like, and how are you and others measuring whether you are succeeding or not? When we started the Net in Huddersfield, I was given three years to see whether this new community, with the aim of reaching unchurched people, would work. After two years I asked the diocese how they would judge whether or not we might continue. There was some silence before they finally admitted that they were clueless about how to do so!

Many fresh expressions of church are now being given between five and ten years to prove themselves, but I think, for the leaders who are starting something new and fragile, the issue of clarifying expectations is really important. We also need to clarify whether the views of those within the new community and its supporters outside are similar to those of the leaders.

I do not think there are any easy or model answers to what success might look like, but I know that, for everyone's sake, it is important to establish some guidelines at the very least. For instance, if you are starting a fresh expression for people who are similar to you, culturally and ethnically, the expectations should be different from those for something that is more radically cross-cultural. Likewise, if you are starting with a team of 100, the expectations should be totally different from those for a team of five. Any criteria also need to relate to your mission focus and the way it is being fulfilled by the new community.

All this needs to come with a healthy dose of realism about connecting with people who have a diminishing contact with church, either personally or culturally. Recent research suggests that, on average, it takes an adult six years to come to faith in Christ (from the first time they express any interest), so our calling is not going to be a 'quick hit' if we are truly to be a missionary church and connect with people whose culture is way outside the traditional churches.

In terms of clarifying what success means, it is especially important to establish to what extent it is to be defined by numbers or finances, and whether other important factors should be included, such as quality of community, depth of community engagement, missionary endeavour and so on. I felt all this very powerfully when I was leading the Net Church, not least because of the realisation that, in starting it, I had unleashed the nightmare possibility that this long-cherished vision and dream might crash and burn. When it was an idea in my head, it was safe from risk and failure. Linked to this anxiety was the secret thought, 'What will people think of me then?' I realised that I needed to name these fears and work through them with the help of others.

The third area where expectations need managing is the role of the pioneer(s) themselves, whether a single pioneer or a small leadership team is pioneering the new community. It is important to clarify the pioneer's role to help them in leading, and also to help whoever is overseeing them. Perhaps the most important clarification required is how much freedom the pioneer has to develop the venture and any spin-off initiatives. I was involved in helping to set up a pioneering role, and we recruited a wonderful woman to plant a new Christian community, but the whole project was brought to a grinding halt by the local churches who wanted to control everything she did and ensure that she was in attendance at countless meetings. Not surprisingly, she left after a couple of years, feeling constrained by their excessive demands of accountability. Of course, we should all be accountable in any leadership role, but there is a real danger in pioneers being micro-managed. They need boundaries as well as support and encouragement, but they must then be trusted to fulfil the pioneering call that God has given them.

Clarifying expectations is particularly important when the pioneer occupies an additional role in a more traditional church setting. The danger is that they will be sucked into the vortex that is church life, so that any space for pioneering is limited to the margins. Again, it is important to put in place some boundaries to give the pioneer space, energy and freedom to pioneer, while ensuring that they do not feel held back from what they really want to do by what they 'have to' do. Problems can arise when a leader is asked to look after a traditional congregation and then pioneer in their spare time. What tends to happen is that the existing work eats up all the time, leaving the pioneer frustrated by having no space for the new work that they really want to do.

There are also expectations around the issue of focus and the mission of the fresh expression. This can often lead to conflict within the pioneering team or with the supporting church. It involves the key issue of who the mission is for. In my experience, it is often the case that pioneers want to be creating a community to connect with people way beyond the church walls, but the pressure is also on to provide a place for disaffected Christians. While there is nothing wrong with creating a safe place for such people, this may not be the calling of the pioneer. This was our area of biggest conflict within the Net Church. I discovered after a year that a small but significant number of people wanted to create a worshipping community for those who were struggling with church. We were too small to have two foci—involving the unchurched and the dechurched—and some hard decisions had to be made.

If expectations provide the most challenging issues for the pioneer, working with the existing church can also present its own challenges. I often hear from pioneers that they feel marginalised and misunderstood by a church that they feel just doesn't under-

71

stand them. This can be very demotivating for the pioneer and leaves them feeling isolated and often angry. They may feel that their work is unappreciated or does not really count as far as the church is concerned. In fact, the pioneer may often feel much more at home outside the organised church than within it, with the danger that the situation can simply reinforce stereotypes on both sides and produce an unnecessary antagonism. The pioneer may feel as if the church is telling them that their calling is an exuberant 'stage' that they will eventually grow out of so that they can become a 'proper' leader—or the church may constantly question the style of the preaching, music or liturgy within the fresh expression.

I think there are two important ways to approach this issue. Firstly, for their own sake, pioneers must ensure that they do not become isolated in their work, feeling that they are on their own and nobody else cares or understands. This is partly why we started the Breakout Pioneer Conference—to give pioneers a chance to gather and find support and encouragement. It is vital for pioneers to meet regularly with like-minded people for mutual support, and I find it really encouraging to see how various networks are developing at a local and national level to enable this to happen. At such gatherings, pioneers can feel 'at home' without having to explain or defend themselves. If you are a pioneer and you don't meet regularly with anybody for this kind of support, please do something about it very soon!

Secondly, pioneers need to understand their responsibility to the wider church, to which we all belong, whether working in a traditional setting or at the edge. It can be very tempting to give up on the church and plough your own furrow, but the different parts of the church need to learn from each other and work together for the glory of God. To use Paul's body analogy from 1 Corinthians 12, we all need each other. Pioneers need to keep explaining to the wider church not only what they are doing but also why they feel called to do it, so that 'pioneering' becomes embedded in the life of the church. This will not just happen but is part of our collective responsibility as pioneers, which we dare not evade, for the future health and unity of the church. This 'go-between' place may not be the location we would choose, but it is vital that we remain deeply involved in conversation about the present nature and future forms of the church.

Default positions

The next issue that pioneers need to be aware of is the 'default position'. This means the basic fallback position that we revert to when something goes wrong, and it is an ongoing reality in church life. The main problem with the default position is that, for most of us, it is an attitude that is buried deep within us. This means that when we feel it is being put under pressure, we can feel very threatened and respond irrationally without understanding why we are reacting in such a way. We all have a default position, and half the battle is recognising that fact. The issue is particularly evident when we are starting something new, as, in more traditional settings, our default position tends not to be so exposed.

When we are involved in a pioneering initiative, acknowledging our personal 'default position' may present us with some emotional and spiritual challenges as we face up to some of our cherished notions of church being scrutinised. I found that many of my shibboleths about worship, preaching, the nature of church, evangelism and community were challenged. It was painful at times to be questioning fundamental issues but it was really valuable to explore what were ecclesiastical cultural additions and what were the timeless truths of the Christian Church.

Challenging the default position of people within the Net Church was also a draining experience, partly because it was hard work helping people to see what was going on inside themselves at such a deep level, and partly because it produced some huge emotional reactions—and I was often the target of these emotions! Yet, for the good of those who may find Christ in the new community, this is a task that has to be tackled for the long-term good of the church. It means being robust enough to make hard decisions and take tough calls. I was convinced of the importance of this many years ago, when I was serving at a church where the main leader ducked any such difficulties and challenges. I saw how the congregation declined, disabled by a variety of unexamined default positions. What is needed is not the formation of a monochrome church but a unity governed by certain core principles, around which everyone can gather for the sake of the whole community. This also emphasises the need for leadership to be plural so that one leader's own default position does not become the only permissible version, and so that there is mutual support and accountability for all those in leadership.

Support and accountability

It will have become clear by now that I think support and accountability for pioneer leaders are crucial, because of the exposure of being on the edge, often with limited resources and uncertainty about the future. When we started the Net Church, one of our first steps was to set up an advisory group to work with us and to provide support and wise counsel. I met with this group of five people four or five times a year, and their help was invaluable, especially when the situation was sticky. Half the members of the group were my choice and the other half were chosen by the diocese. I respected and trusted them and always took their advice (although they were clear that I did not have to). I would always advise anyone starting a new ministry to have some kind of advisory body working with them.

Informal support is also vital for pioneers, and this can be arranged through friends, other pioneers and various networks. It is easy to be so closely focused on our work that we lose a sense of perspective. Others can come alongside us and help us establish a sustainable work/life balance. The critical words of a close and trusted friend are of infinite worth, as you will face lots of criticism that you may find untrustworthy. Find such good people and cultivate your relationships with them. This means prioritising your diary to free up time to be with them. It also means arranging to do fun and creative things with other people, to give ourselves space for recreation. I have now spotted in myself that if I'm not laughing, it is a warning sign of stress. If I have not laughed recently with friends, I know that I need to do something about it, for my own sanity and humanity. Especially in the early days of a pioneering situation, 'the work' can take over, so it is important to establish good relationships and patterns right from the outset. If you do not have such people or places, I strongly suggest that you seek them out, invest in them and allow them to invest in you. The dividends from this will be huge for you and your ministry.

There are many issues that are common to all church leaders, but there are some unique pressures on pioneers, which come from moving into new ground and starting from scratch. As I've already mentioned, this can be a very exposed place in which to live, and we need to understand clearly the challenges we are facing. While pioneers can help each other, those in authority in the established churches also need to understand the challenges and provide support and encouragement for pioneers, so that they survive and thrive. We need to cherish our pioneers, to affirm them and their ministries, and to set them free to complete the work to which God has called them, for the sake of the church and the spread of the good news of Jesus.

For more information on the story of the Net Church in Huddersfield, see David Male, *Church Unplugged* (Authentic, 2008).

5

Nourished for the journey: the pioneer and spirituality

Adrian Chatfield

It sometimes takes an outsider to see the tangle we have got our-selves into over church. Back in 2007, I heard a Nigerian bishop say that the West has turned church into chaplaincy—or, worse still, into a tribe. Whatever the rights and wrongs of his observation, it's a salutary reminder to Christians working in the uncharted waters of pioneer ministry that we cannot always count on the church to nourish our spirits in a way that keeps God's priorities at the forefront. At best, our mission becomes the spiritual care of insiders. At worst, we become the interpreters of the vacuous spirituality of so much inherited Christendom.

Diatribe over! Here's the reality check. When I was ordained, I knew and understood the relatively stable context in which I would exercise ministry. Even then, I thought the world was changing fast, and I remember the impact that Alvin Toffler's *Future Shock* had on me when it came out in 1970. But it was change that I understood—a continuation of the gradual change that has always been with us—so I understood the ministry that was expected of me. It was an inherited model that had worked for generations and still worked in many settings. While I knew that we needed to do more—to evangelise, to offer hospitality, to make the church more 'user-friendly'—it felt like more of the same. Meanwhile, the world was changing beneath my feet, and I hardly noticed...

Alongside this 'brave new world' of change, we need to place the stability of the Christian gospel, where, in a different sense, nothing has changed. We are 'citizens with the saints and also members of the household of God, built upon the foundation of the apostles and prophets, with Christ Jesus himself as the cornerstone' (Ephesians 2:19–20, NRSV), in no way different from the first Christians in Ephesus. To be a disciple of Christ in 21st-century Britain is therefore both the same as, and utterly different from, the experience of the first believers. We need, therefore, to avoid overstating the difference when talking about the spirituality of the pioneer. It is a Christian journey lived in faithfulness to Jesus the Messiah, the same as ever. Our task is to identify facets of contemporary life that create particular challenges and difficulties, as well as offering distinctive joys and opportunities.

Eyes fixed on Jesus

Pioneering ministry is exercised in faithfulness to Jesus, 'the pioneer and perfecter of our faith' (Hebrews 12:2). We have a ministry only because of Christ's sacrificial death and resurrection, and its continuance depends entirely on his grace. As the seductive certainties of culture, church, institution and role fade, we are thrown back entirely on to him. The development of a mature spirituality must be utterly Jesus-centred: responsive to him, nourished by him, dependent and faithful, at home with him, and assured in a deep sense of call.

The proper response to the grace that God has shown us in Jesus is eucharistic: one of deep gratitude and thanksgiving. The energy, thrust and excitement of building the kingdom must be wrapped around a reflective centre: knowing who we are in Christ. Before our public ministry, and after it, we are simply 'in Christ'. Our ministry may sustain us for now, but, on its own, it will soon become an empty vanity. John Wesley, on his way back from his failed mission to Georgia, wrote:

I went to America, to convert the Indians; but oh! Who shall convert me? Who, what is he that will deliver me from this evil heart of mischief? I have a fair summer religion. I can talk well; nay, and believe myself, while no danger is near; but let death look me in the face, and my spirit is troubled. Nor can I say, 'To die is gain!'

JOHN WESLEY'S JOURNAL, TUESDAY 24 JANUARY 1738

The key to this is memory, the 'take care that you do not forget' of the Old Testament (see Deuteronomy 6:12), and memory must be nourished by a return to the texts of our faith and the narratives of our Christian journey. We must remember what God has done for us all and what God has done for each of us, and, in remembering, rejoice and retell the story to all who will listen. The fuel of our passion is our personal experience of Jesus. This fuel is burnt in the fires of testimony and (sometimes) martyrdom.

Deep listening

The story is told of three old men, hard of hearing, on a slow train out of London. As they approached a station, one asked, 'Is this Wembley?' The second replied, 'No, it's Thursday.' Immediately, and with alacrity, the third said, 'So am I; let's get off and have a drink.'

Many voices clamour for our attention, and we also struggle to hear. It is far too simple to say that the only voice we need to listen to is the voice of God. Our spiritual task is to listen to and weigh the many voices, and, in so doing, learn the art of spiritual conversation. The voice of God, the world's many voices, the voice of the people of God and our own inner voice all need to be woven together and heard in relation to one another. In allowing and encouraging these discourses, we stop simply reacting to the demands and noises of the moment, committing ourselves rather to a deliberate, thoughtful act of the will: deep listening.

There is no magic to this art, but there may be some things for us to unlearn, and it is certainly possible to learn the discipline through regular exercise. Its first feature is attentiveness: the time set apart for identifying and listing the voices one by one. Having identified them, the temptation is to regard one of these voices as primary, and the others as distractions from which we need to be delivered by God. We must reject this approach: there is no such thing as a bad voice. It is what we do with the voices that counts.

Pioneer ministry requires that we listen to God in exactly the same way as we do in all ministry: there is no difference. What is new (and may be a lesson for the whole church) is the idea that the contradictory, sometimes strident, often secular or careless voices of the world that bombard us may also be words from the Lord. They are the cries of the needy calling for God, the pleas of the unheard asking to be understood, the voice of the Spirit challenging us to meet people in their marketplaces, not ours.

The second feature of deep listening is discernment, the task of separating the gold from the dross. Discernment demands a patient, waiting spirit—a rare commodity in a busy church. My busyness is often compounded by a fear that I will not meet targets, that I will not fulfil the mission plan in time before the funding plug is pulled. So waiting is a risky business, but there is no substitute for the risks of allowing God to determine the way forward, however costly.

When we give ourselves the 'luxury' of a waiting space, the task of sifting through the sounds of this complex conversation can begin, and there are three tools that aid godly discernment. The first is to ask which parts of what we hear give us consolation, and which have a spirit of desolation about them. Those who are familiar with the Spiritual Exercises of the Ignatian tradition will recognise this tool, but it is inherently simple. God blesses us; he does not curse us. What is truly godly will lift our spirits.

Linked to consolation is the working of our conscience—something currently not much discussed. It may be that we have become jaundiced, knowing how deceitful our conscience can be. It is striking, though, how frequently the apostle Paul writes about it in his letters, and in Romans 9:1 he refers to the intimate link between his conscience and the inspiration of the Holy Spirit. Conscience alone will never deliver us from sin: Macbeth discovered that, to his eternal cost. But those who allow their consciences to inform and challenge their decisions quickly discover how faithful the voice of the unhindered conscience can be to the voice of God.

The limitation of the personal conscience lies in its individualism, and this, for the pioneer, is aggravated by an often necessarily individual or isolated approach to the God-task. It is commonplace to observe that loneliness is one of the greatest spiritual dangers of pioneer ministry, and it must be offset by mentoring. Now there's a quandary here. In these early years of pioneering, there are not enough mentors who have themselves been involved in quite the same way in pioneer work, so who do we turn to? The short answer is that pioneers don't necessarily need pioneers to mentor or accompany them spiritually. They need honest, straightforward, blunt listeners, who are not afraid to challenge them. Just don't choose someone who doesn't get the idea at all! Having said that, there is no harm in having to explain yourself to a relative outsider. It focuses the mind, and the intentions, very well.

Subversive discipleship

David Augsburger's remarkable *Dissident Discipleship*[1] speaks of a 'radically inverted mandate' for living, leading to a new order of

luxurious poverty, impious piety, inverted values and inside outsiders. You'll have to read the book to get the substance of his
challenge, but the underlying message is that everything we do has
upside-down and inside-out energy, because we no longer belong
to the world.

On a good day, we all long to be such disciples, not least in
relation to the frustrating institutional and death-delivering controls
that the church seems to impose upon us. Sometimes the result
is that we act in fretful opposition to the church we love to hate,
assuming that this is what subversive discipleship looks like.

Far from it! The type of subversion to which Jesus calls us is the
subversion of love, the refusal to go along with petty tyrannies and
restraints that choke the spirit, because we care too deeply for the
institution to see it lose its life. It may even be that God has called
you to save the Anglican or Methodist or URC denomination from
itself, and restore it to its bridal splendour. Who knows?

So your subversion comes from God's heart, not your own
agenda. It is very easy to walk away from the tedious acts of worship
offered Sunday by Sunday, on the grounds that we are pioneers.
God, on the other hand, may be calling us to explode inside the
church, not outside. Such subversion is for life, not death.

Discontent

For some, however, there comes a moment when our faithfulness
to Christ requires us to walk away from, or face down, the institution. The great Indian saint Sadhu Sundar Singh (1889–1929) was
converted to Christ while lying on a railway line, waiting for the
approaching express train to end his life. The vision he received led
him to the Bishop of Calcutta, for he now knew that he would serve
his Saviour till his death. At first he expected to serve in the Church
of England in India. He offered himself for full-time ministry, only
to be told of the contracts, boundaries, restraints and controls that

Anglican ordination would wrap around him. In faithfulness to Christ, he refused ordination (and stipend) and spent the rest of his life in itinerant Christian ministry, trusting God to provide the means of ministry, until he disappeared for ever from view in the Himalayas.

Trackless regions

In the days before geo-positioning and sat-nav were commonplace, we were doing some work in the arid northern part of Namibia. In the late afternoon, when the temperature dropped from its high point of about 45°C, my wife and I went for a walk in what we thought was a straight line, for about an hour. The sun dipped, we turned to return, and discovered very quickly that we were walking in circles, in a land where we knew no one and spoke none of the language. I have never known my confidence levels drop so fast, and never been so relieved as when we spotted a hut we recognised.

It is unsurprising that the New Testament never speaks of maps. I think I unconsciously used to read John 14:6 as if it were a mapping exercise, until one day (at a funeral) I found myself saying, 'Jesus never gives us a map of the spiritual journey. He is the map: follow him. You will never know where you are going until you arrive at your destination, but Jesus knows where you need to go.'

This takes us back, in a way, to the first section of this chapter, about fixing our eyes on Jesus, who is the pioneer of pioneers, the mapper and geographer of our faith. But I want to take the idea in a slightly different direction now. In the absence of the certainties of a clear spiritual map, laying out the way forward, the danger of walking in circles needs to be counteracted by a carefully boundaried spiritual life. These boundaries are provided by the patterns and rhythms of a worshipping community, the connectedness of Christian fellowship and the discipline of an ordered rule of life.

I don't say this because I'm good at these things: I'm not. I say them because I have, on countless occasions, counted the cost of walking in spiritual deserts in aimless meandering, rather than with an ordered and contained spirit.

Especially in the early stages of a pioneer project, it is difficult to conceive how we can be nourished by the inherited patterns and rhythms, especially in a setting where there are hardly even the seeds of a new community emerging. What are we to do? Find a local church to go to while our project comes to birth? But isn't this precisely the problem—that we ourselves have not been nourished by the tradition? So many people are pioneers because of personal disenchantment with that tradition.

Yet we do belong: the Church of Jesus Christ to which we seek to be faithful is the one and only Church, and the truths we communicate are those that we have inherited from down the ages, from the earliest times. We belong profoundly to this Church and we need to own and be owned by it. That mutual responsibility is rooted in prayer, and no pioneer ought to launch his or her own 'career' without a backing team. I imagine that most of you who read this chapter can name those people on whom you depend for regular, faithful and committed support in prayer, but the paucity of conversation about 'prayer warriors' in today's pioneering church worries me deeply. If nothing else emerges from this chapter, the revisiting and revision of your backing team must be your first priority. Keep in touch with them; I pray for those who ask me to, but I find it really hard when I never hear back from them.

These people are, in truth, your real church. As they pray for you, you are called to pray with them, and this is where their patterns and your rule of life coincide. In his early life, my father was a member of a religious community, a monk of the Society of the Sacred Mission. It was a community, at one time, of more than 100 people, living together in a Benedictine pattern of stability, chastity and obedience. Some years ago, one member of the community felt that God was calling him to the solitary life, as a hermit. He found a house that would serve as a hermitage in the north-east of England and set himself up there, alone. I remember wondering how it worked, being a member of a community without a community around him.

I now know that he continued, as strongly as ever, to be wrapped around by the community life of his brothers, both through their prayer and by sharing with them the disciplines of their daily life. This included saying the same monastic offices as they did, at the same time and in the same way, not for the joy or the feeling of it but to be kept safe within their boundaries in the trackless wastes of the eremitic life. It is the same for you, and perhaps God is calling you—isolated or remote as you may be—to practise the same worshipping life as that of the Church universal, adapted to your context and circumstances.

One example will put flesh on the bones. One of the few things that Jesus told us to do was to continue to break bread and share the cup in remembrance of his death and in thanksgiving for the salvation that is ours in him. Yet in many new church contexts, this is the one thing that rarely, or never, happens. The fresh expressions of church in early Christian Rome were nourished eucharistically by the seven deacons, who carried the consecrated elements from the central act of worship to the outlying, beleaguered, small groups of saints, and to the sick, if the tradition is to be believed. It may be that the contemporary church is being called to recover this practice in a new way. Should the local Christians in your neighbouring church be feeding you by bringing you the bread and wine of Communion regularly from their shared table? Such an act of hospitality would turn a good idea (Christian community) into a practical reality, give a real sense of belonging and—who knows?—even build bridges between inherited and new church.

A life of blessing

We began by talking about the need to be rooted in Jesus: to remember, and to testify. We end with a call to a life of hope. Some of the new churches that are coming to life through your ministry will flourish and others will fade. They cannot ultimately nourish you, but your faith can. The trouble is that, in the heat of the moment, what you see and spend your time with can become the thing that you lean on, the source of your sustenance. It will fail.

Jesus will not fail. The writer of the letter to the Hebrews reminds us:

In the beginning, Lord, you founded the earth, and the heavens are the work of your hands; they will perish, but you remain; they will all wear out like clothing; like a cloak you will roll them up, and like clothing they will be changed. But you are the same, and your years will never end. (Hebrews 1:10–11)

The hope to which we are called here is nourished by a life of blessing. Bless God; bless the world; bless yourself. Write this too into your rule of life, and act on it.

Bless God (Latin: *benedicere*, 'to speak good of'). During the 1980s, our church used to attend the Bible Weeks run by the Restoration movement, and I remember vividly how irritated I got one day when we sang, over and over again, a four-line chorus whose four lines were all 'What a mighty God we serve'. Tedious in the extreme, it brought out all that is Anglican in me. Yet, strangely, I've never been able to forget that day, and I regularly find myself repeating the words, now not so much with irritation as with a sense of quiet amazement that it is true. Perhaps that chorus isn't as trite as I once thought. So be boring; get talking; start repeating the truths that the world would have us forget or deny. In the midst of the task, find regular space to articulate your amazement at a mighty, glorious, life-giving God.

Bless the world by appreciating it, by enjoying it. It is, after all, God's, and although it has been marred and deeply fractured, we do no one any good service by simply complaining and waiting for the second coming of Christ. There is so much left that bears the hallmarks of God in the ordinary humanity of people, the ordinary beauty of the world, the ordinary simplicity of everyday life, which needs to be claimed for God. Paul invites us, in Philippians 4:8, to think about 'whatever is true... honourable... just... pure... pleasing... commendable'. This is his call to bless the world by relating to it in its fullness, in the way intended by God. Wonderfully, this relationship so often merges into evangelism, because it leads those of little or no faith to ask what it is that gives us joy and hope and a different way of living. But we do it not as evangelists; we do it simply because God's world deserves to be blessed.

Bless yourself: be kind to yourself, perhaps. Don't allow the church to load burdens on you that God never intended. Not least, treat yourself as God treats you, with forgiveness, generosity and an awareness of the value that he sees in you. God has time for you, so have time for yourself. God does not think of you as being consumed by your ministry, so do not consume yourself in ministry. Be faithful, certainly, but be real. Give to yourself as generously as God gives himself to you, and accept the opportunities that come your way to love and be loved. In so doing, you will find yourself more faithfully than ever holding fast to the will of a wonderful, amazing God.

Note

1   David Augsberger, *Dissident Discipleship* (Brazos Press, 2006).

A pioneer's story

The Ordained Pioneer Minister category hadn't been invented when I went to my selection conference, and my curacy was in a traditional urban team parish. I first realised that the online ministry I had been involved in for the previous couple of years was a fresh expression of church when I went to a Fresh Expressions taster day while I was still a curate.

i-church advertised for a new web pastor just as I was finishing my curacy. I had never thought of online ministry as my main calling but, through various twists and turns, I ended up applying for the post anyway and was appointed in June 2008. i-church had been going for about four years at that point, so I was coming into an established fresh expression rather than being involved in starting it up. I had already signed up for the East Midlands Mission-Shaped Ministry (MSM) course, and I started the course and the job at just about the same time. I found MSM enormously helpful and very practical: every single session seemed to contain something that I needed to know just at the point when I needed it.

MSM taught me that the vital first step when you're starting a fresh expression is listening. This proved to be equally important when coming in to lead an existing project. I knew what my personal vision was but I realised that I needed to listen to the community to find out about the shared vision that God had given us.

I wanted to know what had drawn our longstanding members to the project in the first place and what had kept them there. A few people had joined more recently and had quickly become very involved in the community, and I asked them what had attracted them and what they were hoping for. A vision process had been completed just before the previous priest in charge had left, and, although some of the detailed plans were now out of date, the underlying values were clear. From these different bits of listening, it seemed that the calling for us as a community was twofold: to support people who were drawn to deepen their Christian discipleship and to explore the potential for mission in the online context.

Online ministry presents particular challenges because the online environment changes and develops very quickly. In 2004, when i-church started, people still thought of the internet as a place—'cyber space'—which you went to through your computer and where things you might find offline, such as bus timetables and churches, were replicated in a virtual form. By the time I was appointed in 2008, people were using the internet to socialise as well as for information. 'Going online' was no longer an experience that took you into a parallel world of virtual reality but had become an extensions of everyday life for many people.

We don't see i-church as a website but as a community that meets online. We run a community website for members who want to share their discipleship journey, and a public site where anyone can post a prayer, question or comment. We also provide seasonal prayers and resources that can be viewed by anyone: a lot of visitors use our resources and read our forums without joining. Some of us use social networking sites to connect with people who may not want to visit i-church. You need to enjoy social networking for its own sake to do this. People often contact me through Facebook or Skype when they see I'm online and will happily raise quite serious spiritual and personal problems via live chat.

Because people may feel less socially inhibited online, they can behave in ways they would not dream of in face-to-face meetings. People who enjoy flaming (vitriolic personal attacks) and trolling (provoking and joining in arguments) may join Christian sites because it adds to the fun to see people trying to live up to their Christian ideals while under attack. Some people set up false identities and join communities so that they can enlist sympathy for made-up problems and tragedies. Dealing with problems that arise online can be very stressful because it feels as if it is happening in your home, so people may need a lot of support when their community comes under this kind of attack.

As a Christian community, we have to be aware that someone who disrupts our community may be a damaged or unhappy person who needs our understanding and support. Many members of the i-church community are incredibly compassionate and patient in trying to walk alongside difficult people, and it often falls to me as pastor to draw the line and say, 'No more.'

I'm not sure whether I would have been selected for the category of Ordained Pioneer Minister if it had existed when I went forward for selection. I don't see myself as a very bold or adventurous person and, in many ways, this ministry found me. I think the high and low points for me as a pioneer minister are probably very similar to those of any minister. Seeing people's faith grow and their gifts develop is incredibly exciting. I believe it is part of our calling as a pioneering community to develop a viable business model, so the fact that I am unpaid at the moment goes with the territory, but it can be quite difficult not to equate how much I am valued with how much financial support I get. I have all the usual doubts about my own effectiveness, but these are balanced out by occasional moments of glorious certainty that this is what I am 'for'.

According to Mother Julian of Norwich, 'He did not say, "You shall not be tempest-tossed, you shall not be work-weary, you shall not be discomforted." But he said, "You shall not be overcome."' There are many times when I feel tempest-tossed, work-weary and discomforted. But so far I have not been overcome.

Pam Smith is Web Pastor and priest in charge of i-church, the online missional community founded by the Diocese of Oxford in 2004.

6

Leading the way: pioneering women

Lucy Moore

The wide-open plains and prairies awaited them, those pioneering women of the 1800s, as they sold their furniture, packed up their provisions and hauled the family on to a covered wagon to brave hostile Native Americans, coyotes, typhoid, extremes of weather and loneliness. As they journeyed, they discarded more possessions, once precious to them and now meaningless in the fight for survival. They risked children falling off the wagon and being crushed beneath the wheels, losing their way, being attacked by enemies preying on the vulnerable travellers, and hazards like the dreaded buffalo gnat. Arrival at their destination meant backbreaking work, chopping wood for a log house, clearing land, ploughing with little or no machinery, fetching water, cooking, bringing up children far from the help of extended family or friends. Husbands as well as children met untimely deaths, leaving the women even more isolated. As Devona Block wrote of her pioneering sister-in-law, Diana Block, 'She accepted death as a way of life.'

Why did they do it? Perhaps some had a dream of moving from rags to riches. The so-called Pilgrim Mothers and Fathers, a couple of centuries earlier, certainly appear to have been motivated more by hopes of material gain than by a desire for religious freedom.

But some, like the Danish-born Camilla Jacobsen, went from riches to rags, when the authorities decided she had too many clothes to carry across the plains, so threw all but her underwear and a change of dress into the sea. One thing is certain: the vast majority of those pioneering women must have set out on their incredible journeys because they were expected to do so. Their husbands or fathers wanted or needed to break new ground, and the wives and daughters had the privilege of preparing, packing and planning, then of creating a homestead in the wilderness while the men went out to work the mines, goldfields or sawmills to make a living.

Perhaps this is the biggest difference between pioneering women then and now: the choice (though we must also confess to a marked absence of coyotes). Most women of previous centuries have had no choice but to follow where men have led. These days, more than ever before, women who hear a call to pioneering work in God's kingdom have a far greater degree of freedom to follow that call, and more opportunities to do so. This calls for a very definite 'yee-hah' and singing around the campfire. It means that more of God's servants are free to serve him as the people he's made them to be.

But what do we mean by pioneers today? In what sense are women and men doing that melodramatic Boys' Own act that tends to be suggested by the term 'pioneering'? And how can we, as a church, support and encourage the women God calls to this mercifully axe- and plough-free ministry?

A caveat at this stage: this is not a thesis drawing on hours of research among a carefully selected group of women pioneers. I don't have time for that. Nor is it a rant against Men or the Oppressiveness of the Church (what would be the point?). Instead, I want to celebrate what women might contribute to mission and suggest how the church might support and encourage them in order to take the wagonload of God's wholeness in Christ out to wildernesses that might otherwise never be reached. You will forgive the generalisations, I hope, and read this chapter as written by someone who doesn't fit many of the stereotypes herself. (I owe a great deal to Penny Marsh and Annie Naish for their work with me on women in church leadership in 2009.)

What is pioneering? Being the first to do something and opening up the field for others to follow. In the case of the American pioneers, it meant literally opening up the field by felling timber, burning scrub and ploughing. In the case of pioneers in the church today, it's like the Archbishop of Canterbury's favourite definition of mission: 'seeing what God is doing and joining in'. So none of us are pioneers in the truest sense: we're always following where God has already wielded his machete and chased away the raccoons (a very rough interpretation of Isaiah 40:3–4). Sadly, the list of 'innovators' in the Wikipedia entry for that word would leave an alien certain that only men can be innovators: all the early aviators, car designers and inventors of the worldwide web listed are unrelentingly male. But as I believe that this has more to do with cultural conditions than with an inherent and exclusive aptitude of men to be pioneers, women should not be daunted.

Pioneers may or may not be discontented with their status quo. They may see a wilderness of some sort, have a vision of how it could be made a more fruitful place to live, and abandon an old way of life in order to set out on a journey in pursuit of that vision. They may well expect hardships, suffering and isolation but, equally, may have the kind of temperament that thrives on these conditions and predisposes them to prefer an environment in which they make up their own rules, rather than conforming to expectations. They may hand down to their descendants a heritage of coping in adversity, of determination and the ability to be satisfied with very little in material terms. The parallels between them and modern pioneer ministers don't need to be elaborated.

Perhaps, for some of those early American pioneering women, the journey was a fantastic opportunity to leave behind some of the restrictions placed on women at that time, and to discover for the first time who they really were and what they were capable of when they weren't confined to tea parties and flower arranging. As women today are trained and work as pioneers in the church, they have a similar freedom to push back frontiers, rise to challenges and bring their unique insights into the church as a whole, enriching and strengthening it.

If we as a church want every person, male or female, to grow into the fullness of Christ and be given every opportunity to fulfil their calling to 'life in all its fullness' (John 10:10, GNB), what might we consider doing to resource and support women who are called by God to walk into the wilderness and whip out a metaphorical machete? Let's look at the questions of the culture we live in, the church heritage we work in, our readiness to recognise male and female ways of pioneering, the impact of children and home-making and accepted wisdom on how to encourage women.

Should we acknowledge that, despite greater opportunities than ever before, in our UK culture it is still that bit tougher for a woman to be a pioneer than it is for a man? 'Man' is still the default setting, as it were. In UK society, the water in which we swim, men are more likely to be in pioneering roles in business, banking, teaching, arts, health care—almost any sphere of society—than are women. Will the House of Commons ever reach a 50:50 ratio of men to women? Women are still brought up with very subtle messages that to put themselves forward is both pushy and inappropriate. On our breakfast cereal packet, I have observed that the picture of the loathsomely fibre-filled family running along the beach has the small boy at the front reaching out for the football, with his dad inches away, laughingly trying to beat his son to the ball, while Mummy and daughter jog happily behind them, content to let the males compete for the ball. It's subtle; it's trivial; but it's there every morning, reinforcing my sense that my daughter and I belong behind the men, following in their footsteps, avoiding aspiration or confrontation. (A photo of our family would have mother and daughter sprinting in the opposite direction to the football, pioneering their way towards the ice cream stand while father and son argue over who gets the iPod, leaving the dog in gleeful possession of the ball.)

To counterbalance this cultural bias, perhaps churches could consider proactively giving women opportunities, mentoring and encouragement to dream dreams and follow visions. Youth leaders could be asked to take stock of how much attention they give to young women compared with young men. And just to illustrate that this is not a patronising task to set, when I was teacher training in left-wing Oxford in the 1980s, I well remember one lesson we were asked to teach under peer observation. We knew that we were being observed to count how many times we spoke to boys and how many times we spoke to girls, how many times we told off one group or the other, how many times we praised one group or the other. Even with the hypersensitivity that came from knowing which aspect of my teaching was being noted, I was staggered to find afterwards that I had given one group four times as much attention as the other: no prizes for guessing whether it was boys or girls. Try listening to the Today programme on Radio 4 and counting how many men are the subject of the news items compared with women, and how many men are interviewed compared to women. A little positive discrimination in such circumstances can only help to redress the balance.

Not only in society at large is there a cultural bias against women pioneers, but in the heritage of the church there is a history which means that women need an extra bit of encouragement to follow their call. Despite splendid examples of pioneering women in the Bible, like Phoebe (Romans 16:1–2) and Priscilla (Romans 16:3; Acts 18:18, 26), both of whom were prepared to leave home and travel to new territory for the sake of the gospel, some church traditions have dissuaded women from pursuing a pioneering role, perhaps out of a conviction that only men should or can lead. There may be for some women, therefore, a residual guilt that they are 'presuming' to lead, rather than an open-armed acceptance of the role. It's interesting that missionary work has always been acceptable work for a woman, as long as it has been overseas. That can't be because they were 'only' nursing, teaching children or caring for orphans. Mildred Cable, in China, was an evangelist and teacher; and Lottie Moon, frustrated by her role of teaching in a school when she knew herself to be called to evangelism, wrote: 'Can we wonder at the mortal weariness and disgust, the sense of wasted powers and the conviction that her life is a failure, that comes over a woman when, instead of the ever broadening activities that she had planned, she finds herself tied down to the petty work of teaching a few girls?'[1]

Perhaps the church felt that it was permissible for a woman to teach if no one else was prepared to do it—and, as it was so far from home, any ensuing damage would be limited. Centuries of church tradition weigh against women having an equal role in acknowledged, authorised leadership within the church, giving women today a disproportionately small number of female role models. Recognising this and appreciating that women may have less confidence by right of historical precedent is a step towards equality. A confident young woman with leadership potential will hardly want to throw in her lot to a business in which she has no chance of becoming a groundbreaking director, while men of similar capabilities achieve just that. There is still pioneering work to be done in the wildernesses within the church, never mind outside it. If we're interested in creating a just society, we need to be conscious of injustice towards women in our own backyard.

Language may well play a part in excluding, belittling or disabling women's gifting and role, while encouraging only men's. The word 'pioneering' itself, while terribly gung-ho and exciting, conjures up pictures of baggy shorts, bushy moustaches and manly struggles with alligators. We need parity of pay: women are far more likely to be unpaid church leaders than men. We need to insist on parity of voice, making sure that women are fairly represented in the structural bodies of the church, in the lecture hall, on the printed page and on the conference podium. Given that a feminine trait is to 'get on with the job' rather than to seek glory and recognition, it may require extra effort to dig women speakers and writers out of their lairs: they are less likely to put themselves forward. Organisations like the Sophia Network are invaluable sources of great women speakers and mentors.

In the area of recognised ministry, the question arises: what if a man and a woman, faced with several wildernesses, choose different ones in which to do their pioneering work? If the woman chooses a different wilderness from a man, has different priorities from his as she sets about her new life there and creates a different homestead from his, will her homestead be recognised as valid, fruitful and civilised, or will only the man's be seen as worthwhile in the eyes of those who have the structural power? Will her homestead be overlooked, unsupported and ultimately neglected? What if neither the man's nor the woman's is 'better'— just 'different', growing different crops and working in a different way for a different wilderness? Surely it makes sense to support both pioneers and for each to learn from the other?

If a woman sees the deep spiritual need of young mothers, prostitutes or children with special educational needs, and walks into that wilderness, will her work be recognised as being as valuable as cutting-edge evangelistic work among motorcyclists or blokes down the pub? It's very odd that toddler groups have been running for years, yet the average toddler group leader in a church is taken for granted far more than the youth leader, preacher or house group leader. Similarly, children's groups may be run during the week, meeting the needs of unchurched children, but the leaders in this unbroken field may receive little recognition, train-ing or support. Is this because, in the work of bringing up the next generation (traditionally 'women's work'), women are revered as being naturally good at it, so there is no need to invest in their selection, training or development? Or is it because the work itself simply isn't valued? Women may see different wildernesses to bring under the plough: do those with power in a church recognise all wildernesses to be of equal worth?

There may also be a difference in the way a woman organises what she has pioneered. An emphasis on relationships and emotional intelligence rather than hierarchy and numbers may come into play: a woman pioneer might run a team very differently from a male pioneer. Does the church see both styles of leadership as valid? Are people who pioneer in quiet ways invited to speak at conferences, write books, join steering groups, and sit on decision-making committees?

Going back to the subject of children, what value does the church place on the creation of a home in which to bring up our own children? If a pioneer woman abandoned the next generation and worked only in the wilderness, the settlement would be very short-lived. This is an extract from the diary of a 19th-century missionary, Mary Richardson Walker:

Rose about five. Had early breakfast. Got my house work done about nine. Baked six loaves of bread. Made a kettle of mush and have now suet pudding and beef boiling. I have managed to put my clothes away and set my house in order. At nine o'clock pm was delivered of another son.[2]

Pioneering women in the 19th century gave birth in appalling conditions, brought up children in situations of extreme duress, coped with the agony of children dying in the harsh environment they had come to, and did all that while farming, building and cooking because they had no choice. Pioneering is tough and demanding on families, and, to state the obvious, women bear children. In our culture it may be more common than it used to be for men to take an equal share in child care, but it is still overwhelmingly more usual for a woman to take on the lion's share. It is no coincidence that many male pioneers in the church are in the 25–40 age bracket—an age when many women are coping with babies and toddlers all day and for much of the night, and have little time or energy left for carving out cultivation in a spiritual wilderness. Doubtless, if there was no choice, they would manage just as their ancestors did, but to deliberately opt for that sacrificial way of life—sacrificial on the part of the children as well the women—would be a huge undertaking. Could a church affirm the role of those pioneers-by-nature who have chosen to bring up their children, and help them to see the pioneering opportunities open to young parents that are closed to the rest of the church, so that they can continue to be the people they were created to be during a career break? Women often have to juggle family and training for pioneering ministry, whereas men often just do the training: anecdotal evidence suggests that training is doubly hard for many women to get through. Conference organisers and ordinand training bodies need to value the crucial role of parenthood and make it easier for women (and men) to fulfil both callings more easily. Child care provision, timing of sessions and expectations of early morning or early evening work would be good places to start making changes.

One piece of accepted wisdom in the encouragement of women is that women respond well to role models. As I have pointed out already, there are fewer pioneering women, historically, for women to be inspired by. But an interesting question is whether pioneering women really need role models. After all, if Mary-Beth or Carrie-Lou has already carved a path across the prairie and you are inspired by her example to blaze a trail yourself, isn't she the pioneer, rather than you? At the pearly gates, I don't expect to be told that I can't come in because I never became a Josephine Butler, a Hannah More or a Jackie Pullinger, when all I was called to be was me. Maybe it is all too common a female trait to be too scared to set out where no one has been before, to be too deferential, too cowardly to take risks and fail. Perhaps more women should delight in the lack of role models, as the possibilities ahead of them are then limitless. But for those who are inspired to blaze their own trail by the example of a sister in the faith, we can also provide role models of pioneering women for the next generation and tell their inspirational stories with pride. Women respond well to encouragement and affirmation, too: as a church, we need to build that affirmation into the system rather than depending on a pastorally sensitive elder or bishop to happen to give it.

Let me introspectively ponder a while on my own role. I suppose, in a small way, I am a pioneer through my work with Messy Church, albeit unordained and accountable only to the company I work for rather than to an ecclesiastical authority (and I am certainly a woman). What is it that has enabled and empowered me to carry out and, yes, enjoy this role so much? What has helped me become the person God made me to be through it? I have a partner who sees jobs that need doing to run a house, rather than roles that need filling in the house. When I wasn't working outside the home, I did the cooking; now either of us does the cooking. I am a dab hand with clingfilm, though it drives him demented; I panic at the sight of a new piece of software, while his eyes light up. The fact that the children are now old enough to be left for longer periods is a huge factor affecting what I am able to do. Workwise, it is significant that I have a line manager who values me as a person, not just for the work I do; who rings up for a chat to find out how I am, not just to set tasks or chivvy about deadlines. I am part of a team of peers who offer prayerful support and knowledgeable advice or sympathy. There's an ethos within the organisation I work for that encourages reasonable risk-taking and accepts that this might entail failure as well as success. I receive an equal salary to my colleagues in similar roles, men and women. It's been a great help, especially during the many times when I have felt useless, to belong to the Fresh Expressions Associate Missioners Team and to receive affirmation from the leadership team there. It has also been a real help not to have to worry about maintenance of church buildings and structures but to be free to create new networks and ways of supporting people involved in Messy Church. Similarly, the freedom to spend time thinking, talking, listening, planning and praying has been invaluable.

I suppose that what I have appreciated most has been the opportunity to let the work develop in a me-shape: yes, it has Christ at the centre all the way, but I mean that my personality works with God and with the job to grow the kingdom. This is a privilege I recognise in a world where many people who are intricately carved pegs are forced into rough-and-ready holes.

Has being a woman been a disadvantage at all? I suppose there's an element of frustration at being stereotyped: Messy Church involves children and families, which is traditionally a concern of women in the church. It would have been good to have been a man pioneering in this particular field, giving men implicit encouragement to see it as a crucial area of mission. Also, given that I spend much of my life shifting furniture round church halls and lugging heavy boxes of crafts and books around with me, a man's physique would have been very handy. But I can honestly say that apart from that, my gender hasn't been a problem. Had I been through more orthodox training or been ordained, I might have told another story: as it is, being a bishop is not on the agenda anyway.

I quoted earlier from the sister-in-law of Diana Block, an early American pioneer. This is the full quotation: 'Because she accepted death as a way of life, her joy for the newborn has been multiplied.' Pioneer ministry, ordained or not, involves accepting death as a way of life. For some, it might mean dying to some learned or inborn 'female traits' that prevent women from seeing or exploring their own wilderness: traits like fearfulness, deference, wanting to please, not wanting to be seen as pushy. For others, it might mean letting go of prejudices about what women are capable of doing or being; it might also mean letting old models die and learning to appreciate different styles of working, re-evaluating what success might look like. But all these small deaths are died in order to bring life: fruitfulness in the wilderness of our own lives, the lives of communities in which we are called to work, and in the church that nourishes us and sends us out. Pioneering women of the 19th century had it tough, but the true pioneers among them thrived on the hardships, as true pioneers still do today. After all, when did God ever promise his people an easy ride?

Notes

1 Lottie Moon, article titled 'The Woman's Question Again' (1883).
2 Mary Richardson Walker, *Diary*, 16 March 1842.

Details of pioneering women from Notable Women Ancestors can be found at www. rootsweb.ancestry.com/~nwa/pioneer.html

A pioneer's story

It was probably natural that I should become a pioneer. My parents had pioneering spirits, so I think it's probably in my DNA: I do things 'outside the box' and push boundaries. I look for adventures and creative ways of doing life. And, since my life is founded upon my faith, then church life is unlikely to be an exception.

The high points far outweigh the low points, as far as I am concerned. My highest point was when my friends agreed to work with me! I believe in relational church and love working with like-minded people in a team. At Thirst, the café community that I lead in Cambridge, we are from different social backgrounds and display the variety that is the kingdom of God. I love watching the process over time of people discovering God's interest in them. When this happens, I feel my heart do somersaults: it's a 'high' like no other. It is always a low point though, when people walk away. I have learnt over the years not to take such things personally, so although I am sad when it happens, I no longer worry that it's because of something I have done or said. At Thirst we are not afraid to criticise ourselves constructively, so we can look at why people move on. We want Thirst to be an attractive place that draws people to God's love as they see loving relationships in action.

As a pioneer, though, the biggest low for me personally is lack of time and energy to do all that is in my head and heart to do. The leadership team I work with are really patient with me, as I have new ideas and initiatives on a weekly basis. Everybody at Thirst plays an important part, yet often our ideas don't get beyond dream-sharing as we are unable to initiate many of the things we want to do because of lack of time and resources. We always pray a lot before we start any new initiative, however. I like the idea of counting the cost before starting the building.

Thirst meets on a Friday morning because weekends are family time for most people, and we gather in the school lounge. We regularly have about 15 people, plus children at different places in their journey of faith. Many have no previous experience of church at all. I am fascinated to see how their reasons for not having previously gone to church are nearly always connected to their own fears. Some feel that they would not be accepted, while others are afraid that they won't know what to do at church. Another fear is that their children might misbehave, so that they would meet with disapproval. Interestingly, in three years I have yet to meet with anyone who has a problem with or fear of God. Maybe the problem is how we 'do' church—or, at least, people's perceptions of how we 'do' church.

It is fantastic to watch people seamlessly become part of the church as they are drawn into our faith community. Fears are broken down in a natural way through welcome and acceptance. We have testimonies, Bible studies, prayer times, Eucharists, and the proclamation of the word in a variety of creative ways. We are a worshipping community that is growing and learning together; people are on a journey of faith. I think one of my highest points was when one of our community made a comment about us being the church, and then hastily looked at me and enquired, 'We are the church, aren't we?' Thirst doesn't obviously look like church, as most people think they know it!

Since pioneering Thirst, I have began training as an Anglican Pioneer Ordinand at Ridley Hall, Cambridge, although I come from a Pentecostal charismatic background. I have been asked why I am bothering with ordination, since I already have a Bible College training and have pioneered an initiative. Firstly, I believe it is important to belong to something that has a far wider-reaching context. I am aware, as a pioneer, of my own vulnerability. It is important for me to be grounded in a larger community of faith, especially since I have pioneered independently. Secondly, I am by nature independent and creative, and I think it is important to be accountable to others in a safe place outside my own environment. The Anglican Church has much to offer me and I can offer my gifts to the wider community. It is diverse enough to embrace my gifts without trying to suppress my calling as a pioneer. I have enjoyed learning from colleagues at Ridley who are training for traditional forms of church, as well as the other pioneers. I hope I can encourage and build them up in their ministry too, and be a resource to the wider church in the future.

It costs to pioneer, both personally and financially, but we always seem to have what we need. A missionary I once knew said, 'Money should never be a reason why you don't pursue what God is asking you to do', and this has proved true over the years. God has provided for us at Thirst, although I suppose a disadvantage for a pioneer in some situations might be the lack of a stipend. My story of pioneering is not necessarily one of hardship and difficulty, but I believe that this is because I am blessed to be part of a great team. I have the support of my diocese and an experienced and encouraging training supervisor, as well as my husband, who is in ministry himself and understands my enthusiasm and excitement.

Thirst's foundations are those of a praying community of friends. I don't believe there is any shortcut to pioneering. We have to be people of prayer who are relational, patient, forgiving, loving, accepting, creative and, most of all, unafraid to take risks and push boundaries.

Sue Butler is planting Thirst Café Community in a school in Cambridge while training as an Ordained Pioneer Minister.

7

Breaking free from individualism: discipleship and community

Peterson Feital

'What matters is the quality of the life to which the disciple is called.'[1]

In the 21st century, the effects of individualism within Christian communities have almost erased the call to true corporate disciple-ship, because now people seek a world tailored to their own personal needs and preferences. As a result, mission has moved away from a natural sharing of Christ in our daily lives, to methods and programmes, with faith being confined to an individual experience as opposed to a life shared. The consequence is the decline of the church.

Even in apparently successful growing churches it has been realised that mission is resulting in converts—'consumer Christians' —who are not disciples. As Mark Greene and Tracy Cotterell write:

One of the primary reasons for our decline is not that society has changed—though it has—but that on the whole in today's churches we don't make disciples, we make converts. We don't make apprentices of

Jesus, people who are moving forward in their ability to live the life of Christ in every aspect of their lives and to show and share that life wherever God has placed them. Furthermore, a disciple is not just someone with a concern for personal holiness and integrity or for evangelism; he or she has a desire for all that is on the Lord of all's agenda. Disciples, then, are called to be the yeast, agents of transformation seeking to see Christ's Kingdom come in every aspect of human culture—intellectual and emotional, economic and artistic, political and domestic, local and global, private and public. [2]

Without an intimate community in which to grow, individual converts are being rendered static in their faith and ineffective in their witness. In the Methodist Church, the Class Meetings, which were to disciple people through modelling prayer, accountability and Bible study with life application, and the Band Meetings, which were to foster outreach and evangelism, have long since disappeared from church, along with the community aspect. The mechanism of discipleship has been lost and the denomination is consequently in serious decline. Without a close-knit community, people do not get to know each other's needs, Christian journeys, families and so on. If church only constitutes a once-per-week one-hour service, it is possible to remain superficial with one another. But, of course, this is not a Methodist problem alone!

Many leaders recognise that it is important for the church to contextualise itself and create an ambience in which the unchurched can explore spirituality. However, there is an equally important challenge, which is to create a community where the marks of being a disciple can be learnt through both teaching and example, such as repentance, suffering, servanthood, selflessness, holiness, discipline, being filled with the Holy Spirit, and being a community-focused people.

Stuart Murray, in his book *Post-Christendom*, re-examines church mission and the challenges for the church in the 21st century. He encourages leaders today to look at the 16th-century Anabaptist movement as providing 'one of the primary paradigms for radical Christians and Christian communities.'[3] Although much has been written on the differences between Anabaptists and the Magisterial Reformers and their political views, little attention has been given to the community aspect of the movement.

The Anabaptists wanted to return to early church patterns of Christian life, with the concept of church as discipleship within a close-knit family.[4] For them, faithfulness to the message of the gospel meant opposition to the patterns of the world. They directly opposed the Christendom (Constantinian) 'system' of the rest of the church at that time, which enforced Christianity as the official religion, resulting in nominal Christianity. Their lifestyle of holiness and accountability to one another meant that they were taken as radicals for not conforming to the church's perception of Christianity. The Anabaptists were preoccupied with the outcomes of truly following Jesus, whatever the personal cost; they trusted the gospel to make a difference in their social life in the community. This was their understanding of mission and their interpretation of the commission to 'make disciples of all nations' (Matthew 28:19).

'Something else'

I believe that the call to make disciples is about witnessing each other's development through growth and through stumbling, just as the first disciples did. Not only is this the way Christians should live, but it is the way the church is meant to grow, from small localised communities where the members act as agents of transformation.[5] A place where closeness is permissible attracts people, Christians and non-Christians alike, because it involves acceptance, belonging and sharing. As it says in Acts 2:47, the early believers were 'praising God and enjoying the favour of all the people. And the Lord added to their number daily those who were being saved'.

In my job as evangelist at St Giles Church, Nottingham, I was asked to create a space for the 15–30 age group. I was given free rein with a Sunday night service that, for a while, had been unsuccessful in attracting this age group, called 'Praise and Prayer'. My first task was to discern God's vision for the age group. In my first six months, I spent time with lots of unchurched people at local pubs, wine bars, schools, universities and the libraries, talking and listening to them. Something became clear to me: these people would not come to a service called 'Praise and Prayer' primarily because the language was not accessible to them; secondly, there was nothing attractive, interactive or personal about its title or its format. These people would not come into the church community unless the church changed its mission approach. The church needed to be willing to take the risk and try something new.

In order to engage with the unchurched, I first had to attract a team of motivated Christians who would join the vision. I wanted to overcome cultural and subcultural barriers between the church and my assigned age group by building a committed team to model a community. A year later, I had a team made up of twelve people who were students, young professionals, an artist, entrepreneurs and musicians. Most of these Christians were people I had met through my constant presence in the community, who captured the vision. Others came simply because they had heard about the vision through the church or were looking for a church themselves.

At this point, our first decision was to change the name of the service—since this would be the entry point for many non-Christians into the Christian community—from 'Praise and Prayer' to 'Something Else'. The reason was very simple: a lot of non-Christians feel embarrassed to tell people about their journey of faith, never mind admitting that they are going to church. As a result, they end up lying about what they are doing. Therefore, if the service was called 'Something Else', people were able to respond to social invitations from their friends with something like, 'I'm sorry but I can't come because I have something else to do' or 'I have something else on', without having to be dishonest or ashamed!

My vision was not to operate like a business enterprise, with targets and so on. I wanted a group of people who had heard the call to be disciples and I wanted to create a community like a close-knit family. The team's aim was to build this community together. For this to happen, we had to pray that each one of us would have inbuilt value and gifting as participants in the community, and in this way we would serve one another. For my wife Helen and I, this meant deciding, even before the team was formed, to practise the gift of hospitality by making our home an open house for anyone at any time. We had been given a beautiful cottage to live in, right next to the church. It meant the giving of our time, and, in the English context, this was countercultural, since most people are often too busy to give personal time to people other than their friends and family.

I had to make a continuing decision that people were more important than my diary and therefore I would drop almost anything I was doing every time someone knocked at the door. It was not easy all of the time, but it was the price that we had to pay. I had other ministerial responsibilities; for much of the time Helen had a full-time job, and I was doing a part-time MA. After a year and a half, we had a constant flow of visitors who came for meals, Brazilian coffee, or just a chat and a laugh, which gradually resulted in conversations about their spiritual journeys or just the English's favourite topic, the weather. If people came while we were having dinner, they joined in, and before too long they were washing up, cleaning and organising birthday parties in our house for other people without telling us! They ranged from unchurched people I had met in the local community to those looking for a church, to some of the church members who had caught the community vision and just loved the Brazilian hospitality and vibe!

Helen and I and the team shared our lives with each other and with these new people, eating together, having coffee together, going to places together, worshipping together and praying together.

We had innumerable parties, which attracted friends of friends. One thing that we were very good at was partying and having a good laugh. As time went by, and as relationships became stronger, the barriers of individualism and reserve started to came down and people spoke about their fears, doubts and challenges. One thing that made me really proud of the community was that no one was judgmental; instead, we were very aware of each other's shortcomings.

During the four years that we stayed there, we witnessed people overcoming eating disorders, reassessing their relationships and providing financially for those who were in need, and we witnessed people being transformed and becoming very confident about their faith.

As part of my ongoing vision to disciple people, and in order to nurture the community, each year we had two teaching blocks during the 'Something Else' service on the marks of being a disciple. Something Else was designed to be a meeting point for the whole community to learn together with a focus on life application. It was an opportunity for those within the community, as well as newcomers, to hear about and process together the meaning and challenges of the Christian walk, individually and corporately. The setting included a welcome of good coffee, a variety of cakes, soft lighting and good background music, in order to make it relaxed and accessible. There were various styles of seating, including pews at the back and sides, small tables and chairs, and cushions on the floor. The team led the service and other members of the community were asked to lead interactive prayers at the end of each talk. Other people were involved and used their gifts, from serving coffee to providing artistic input. The talks were very short—15 minutes maximum—in order to allow time for discussion and personal reflection, and there were various speakers, including church leaders and other leaders from around the country, to bring different insights to our context. The language of worship and Holy Communion was contemporary in order to engage effectively with the age group, and the sharing of testimonies was frequent to encourage and inspire the rest of the community.

Something Else was not meant to be the sole teaching platform but was just one instrument of corporate discipleship alongside everything else we did within the community context. Without the community environment and interactive nature of the service, Something Else would have been demoted to no more than a theoretical learning experience, with too much focus on individual responses and little or no outworking within the corporate life of the church community. This would have damaged our sense of togetherness and supported our individualistic habits, compartmentalising our understanding of Christian community.

Bishop Steven Croft writes:

Although Jesus welcomes and cares for everyone who comes to him, from individuals to great crowds, all the Gospels tell us that he calls out particular individuals to leave everything and to follow him. As is clear from numerous passages, the vocation of the disciples is not only to a series of individual relationships with Jesus but to life in a missionary community. They are in relationship with one another in times of learning, leisure, fellowship and support, and in mission.[6]

The challenge is to break down barriers caused by individualism, with an emphasis on sharing life together daily, including going to a service once a week.

In addition to the regular service, there were three annual 'Something Else' events focused on outreach: Christmas, Easter and Freshers' Week, when new undergraduates arrived in Nottingham. These provided alternative entry points into the church community. Two of the most successful were the Salsa Party and The Journey, which was a contemporary presentation of the Easter story intended to reach people who had never been into a church, to explain, simply and vividly, what happened and why, in a mixed-media exhibition.[7] We also organised an 'open house' setting in a pub for those who were searching for spirituality out-side a church context.

At that time, we had a congregation at the Something Else service varying between 35 and 65 people. We established three weekly small groups to nurture (a) newcomers to the church, in order to teach about the marks of being a disciple; (b) established Christians, to bring them into maturity; (c) people on the fringe, offering a no-pressure environment in which they could discuss their questions about what it means to be a Christian. These small groups provided deeper times of learning, which, as people grew and matured in their faith, fed into and matured the community as a whole.[8] What could have been a once-per-week service became a community of disciples. It was about belonging, and it was about serving and owning the vision.

Here are some of the things participants have said about the community:

Something Else was like an enterprise that didn't offer a conventional faith-building programme. In fact, it was more like a party... there was a sense of restrained and confident chaos, but we all had a feeling that, like any good party, it was up to us (the partygoers, not the event's organisers) to make it work. We learned an awful lot from hearing others' testimonies and journeys, and praise of God followed naturally. Speaking personally, interest and belief in me and what I could do generated my confidence in me and a reciprocal interest in other people and their abilities and journeys. My faith became more real, because it wasn't a Sunday ritual-based belief... it was practical and people-based. (Jenny, artist)

The Something Else community changed my life immediately because it provided me with friends and a spiritual family within weeks of mov-ing to a new city and starting a professional career. (David, radio presenter)

Although many great things happened, I do not wish to make it sound easy. We constantly had to reassess our approach, and this caused tensions because, within the team, we all had different views. In our leadership group we had an equal voice, so sometimes we went for what the majority wanted, displeasing the minority, and sometimes vice versa. From where I stood, it was important for the leaders as a group to have ownership, thereby making the community sustainable.

The most important element was that we welcomed people who looked very different from us. Some drifted away because they found that the price of being committed to their faith and community as well as being missional was a step too far. Others found the challenges of community too much and went to find a church that was more like what they were used to.

Importantly, the vision was embraced by the vicar of the church, whose own family was equally community- and hospitality-orientated: I believe that it is important to have a point of reference and accountability. One thing I realise in retrospect, however, is that after three years we should have moved the Something Else service out to a neutral venue. Some people were happy to be in the community and wanted to make a further commitment but found going to a service in a church building offputting and alienating.

Notes

1   J.H. Yoder, *The Politics of Jesus* (Eerdmans, 1972), p. 38.
2   Mark Greene & Tracy Cotterell (eds.), *Let My People Grow: Making disciples who make a difference in today's world* (Authentic, 2006), pp. 14–15.
3   Quoting H.A. Snyder, *The Radical Wesley* (IVP, 1980), p. 111.
4   Or 'brotherhood': 'Brothers in Christ came to the understanding that the Church consisted of members who made a covenant with God… to love one another, to take up their cross daily and to follow Jesus as Lord of their lives' (www.anabaptistchurch.org: last accessed 20.03.2010)
5   See Matthew 13:33: 'He told them still another parable: "The kingdom of heaven is like yeast that a woman took and mixed into a large amount of flour until it worked all through the dough"' (NIV).

113

6 Steven Croft, *Transforming Communities* (DLT, 2002), p. 133.

7 www.leapoffaithministry.org

8 See Ephesians 4:13: '... until we all reach unity in the faith and in the knowledge of the Son of God and become mature, attaining to the whole measure of the fullness of Christ.'

8

Form and freedom: creating pioneering worship

Adrian Chatfield

Pioneers in the Christian tradition are launching out into new and unexplored places, but not to satisfy their entrepreneurial drive or develop novelties. They are pioneers out of a sense of passion for the gospel, faithfulness to a God who wants that good news taken into new and unlikely places, and frustration with a church that seems to have settled into comfortable middle or even old age.

That said, pioneers return frequently to first principles. Don Carson has famously said that 'if the heart of sinfulness is self-centredness, the heart of all biblical religion is God-centredness: in short, it is worship.' If the tone of this is slightly negative, we might want to add that worship is 'all that we are, delighting in all that God is'. It is a focused way of expressing our loving and obedient response to a God with whom we are in faithful and exclusive covenant. In our postmodern, individualised age, it is probably also necessary to say that Christian worship is primarily corporate, plural: the covenant is between a God and his people, not a God and solitary persons.

Acts of worship in the Old Testament display a number of key features:

- The presence of God is recognised, named and acknowledged as absolutely superior.
- The acts of God among his people and through the course of history are remembered as salvation-stories and proclaimed: there is a narrative quality to worship. We tell God's story and our stories together.
- Worship is full of amazement at the power of God, his unpredictability and sovereign nature, his grace and undeserved mercy. It is characterised by celebration.
- The people of Israel were under no illusion that they were perfect, although they often (and wrongly) felt self-righteous about their status. But their worship displays a penitent quality: worship includes repentance in response to the holiness of God.
- Coupled with repentance is thanksgiving, stemming from gratitude for forgiveness given and grace offered again and again in the face of their stiff-necked stubbornness.

In practice, the worship of this people is a constant approach to the God who has shown that he is on their side. They listen to his word variously communicated, both orally and then in written form; they act on his word, giving him what they believe he wants (sacrifices) and asking (begging) him to fulfil their needs or wants. In the midst of this, their worship often approximates to a battle, as in the case of Elijah on Mount Carmel (1 Kings 18).

These principles always and inevitably come 'dressed in clothes'; there is no such thing as 'naked worship'—which is what a lot of evangelicals are subconsciously hinting at when they complain about 'liturgy' or formalism. When Jesus spoke to the Samaritan woman about worshipping in spirit and in truth (John 4:24), he was not decontextualising worship. He was simply locating it in himself and universalising it. Salvation is for all, and not dependent on any particular mountain. It may, of course, be found on that mountain just as well as elsewhere!

Although worship is always 'dressed', the responses of God's people are condemned when they are empty of content. Properly used, however, the forms of worship are entirely appropriate: sackcloth and ashes in time of great sin; Jacob's altar anointed with oil as an acknowledgment that God is present; various sacrifices made because 'God is worth it'. At their best, these forms are outward and visible signs of an inward response to God's grace.

The unity of the testaments means that this Old Testament approach to worship is still significant, not merely as an illustration of the new or as the predecessor of 'real' worship, but actually so, with certain modifications:

- All acts of repentance are transferred from the partial active sacrifices of the people to the cross of Christ, which is a complete sacrifice in which we are not participants but recipients. At the cross we are completely passive, accepting what God has done for us.
- The remembering which is the centre of our worship is brought up to date: all the salvation stories now point towards the cross, the crux of all salvation history.
- The worshipping people are no longer delimited by the ten northern and two southern tribes. The dividing wall of hostility has fallen; the Holy Spirit has been poured out on all flesh.

Otherwise, the intention and pattern of worship does not change: God is still God. The components that are not modified are re-modelled by the new covenant understanding of a trinitarian God, enriched, completed and fulfilled: 'Glory be to the Father, through the Son, in the Holy Spirit...'

It is sometimes said, or assumed, that a major difference between Old Testament and New Testament worship is that the former is ritual and the latter is ethical. That assumption depends on partial

117

readings of both testaments, which assume that the rituals of the Old Testament are always under condemnation, that there are no ethical demands in Old Testament worship or that New Testament worship is entirely inward, with no outward expressions.

The unity of the two testaments of scripture constantly reminds us, however, that our vocation is:

- to 'worth-ship': the act of considering God, more than others, worthy of praise, honour, respect or devotion. This 'more than' moves from a relative 'you are a God above all gods' to an absolute comparative: all other gods are but idols.
- to lift God up by our words, our actions, our reverence and respect, our humility and our service.
- to lift God up dutifully, because we are in a relationship of obedience and service which requires that worship.
- to lift God up joyfully, because we are in a relationship of dependence and trust, which brings security and engenders gratitude.

As pioneers, we are not in the business of being apologists for a particular form of worship or approach to worship. We are in the business of worship itself, and in our ministry there will always be a longing to see a community of faith emerge, whose expression of love towards God will lift him up in worship, proclaim him in mission and serve the community in faithfulness. Although we may have some ideas in the back of our mind, we will not be able to anticipate exactly what the worship of a fresh expression of church will look like. We understand that it will necessarily be faithful to the principles we have outlined of recognition, memory, proclamation, amazement, celebration, repentance and thanksgiving. But is there anything else that we can expect from this emergent church?

I believe that there are some common-sense human principles that God has built into the way we operate as human beings, which are also key principles. They are hinted at in all sorts of ways in the scriptures, but let us accept them as givens. They can be described as polarities or creative tensions, and include:

- a balance between creativity, freedom and spontaneity on the one hand, and the need for structures, patterns, forms, boundaries and rhythms of life on the other.
- a place for individuals with the core community of faith. Personality, diversity, difference and life circumstances demand space for us to 'be ourselves' in relation to others within the church.
- the axes of transcendence and immanence. God must never be trivialised or seem to be too close or too easy to access, but, at the same time, he is nearer to us than our jugular vein (to misquote a Sufi proverb).
- horizontal and vertical axes to our worship. While, obviously, worship is offered to God, God does not expect us to be neglectful of one another. In fact, within the church we should be modelling what it means to be truly human. Christian worship, therefore, includes the wider perspective of hospitality and deep human relationality. Pioneers must have a vision for worship that is familial, welcoming, homely, fun and deeply challenging.
- the practices of giving/offering and receiving/accepting. Some evangelicals, properly emphasising the all-sufficient character of grace, claim (improperly) that Christians have nothing to bring to worship except themselves. The reality is entirely different. God delights in receiving from those whom he loves, though he does not need to receive from them. In worship, we certainly receive grace from God, but we also give; we create; as artists we share with God in his work of remodelling the world. We bring art, music, dance, drama, bread, wine, dinner parties, computers, motorcycles—the stuff of life.
- the need for worship to be both inculturated and counter-cultural. The clothes of worship, of which we have already

119

spoken, are cultural, and can be described as a sort of language. It may be that some languages are richer than others: it is said that English has the largest vocabulary of any, about half a million words. That doesn't make English the best or most efficient language. Language works when the speaker and the listener both understand it to some degree. So it is with worship. Whatever those who facilitate worship aim to communicate must be understood to some degree, at some level, however intuitive.

At the same time, worship must communicate the values of the kingdom of God, not the kingdoms of this world. Otherwise, it has no gospel power at all. If we use the Eucharist (Holy Communion) as an example, the cultural language of meal is central there. The way in which we celebrate Communion must look sufficiently meal-like to be received as a meal. At the same time, the meal must be (to use but one example) much more inclusive and welcoming than all other human meals, or it will not put the world's hospitality in the shade.

• the tension between the fact that some are gifted to lead worship, but worship is led by the whole people. There is no longer a priestly caste of exclusive worship leaders. Originally, the word 'liturgy' referred to an act or work carried out by the whole people, and, in Christian worship, no one is an observer. At various levels, and with different degrees of commitment, all must be active participants. So those who facilitate through skilful leadership of our liturgies and acts of worship must do so in a way that sets people free and gives them a sense of belonging, involvement and satisfaction.

Given these biblical principles, and the polarities that we have listed, is there a starting point—as a community of faith begins to emerge in some shape or form—for the worship of that community? Certainly the starting point is not, 'Here is the package.' Emphatically, the starting point is not, 'This is what our denomination or chosen pattern allows.'

Worship evolves gradually as a community is formed. I am, in many ways, still a convinced Anglican, persuaded of the value of the inherited patterns and rhythms of the tradition as well as the importance of not interpreting pioneering as a maverick opportunity to be a Christian karaoke artist. At the same time, and more strongly, however, I am persuaded that liturgical structures rarely keep up with changing spiritual and cultural needs. There is an ongoing dialogue between the inherited patterns and the need for those patterns to be stretched, sometimes almost beyond recognition, re-establishing them eventually under the same principles but properly re-inculturated.

This evolutionary uncertainty demands of the pioneer a spiritual rootedness, about which we have spoken in the chapter on spirituality. It also calls for 'liquid worship', set within a relatively formal core, and collaborative worship design. The product (if this isn't too mechanical a term) needs to be mission-shaped. Let me say something about each of these qualities in turn.

Spiritual rootedness

We know that we cannot know where we are going, so our stability lies in being known by God and knowing him. It once was possible, and very seductive, to find one's identity in a particular inherited model of church: this was never appropriate and is entirely impossible for the pioneer. Even denominational identity is up for debate, and the question needs to be asked firmly (though in a godly way), what the future currency of our denominations is in a post-Christian world.

Strangely, in such an uncharted setting, our spiritual rootedness lies in remembering, belonging, mentoring and accountability. We are called to remember the great works of God, testified to in scripture and in our own lives. We are called also to remember the deep traditions of the church, of which worship is a core component.

It is best to illustrate this by way of an example. Over the past 50 years, many new Christian 'churches' have been born out of the evangelical tradition of Western Christianity. Despite a long and honourable tradition of frequent Holy Communion in that tradition, many contemporary expressions of Holy Communion are excruciatingly embarrassing, theologically thin and dramatically understated. The reasons for this are historical: many evangelicals still fear the Catholic 'brand'. Even where this is not so, many new church leaders have little experience or memory of what went before, or experienced it as dry and irrelevant in a pre-Christian phase of their lives, so it is easily dismissed. I remain unconvinced that pioneering requires a rejection of ancient traditions. What is much truer to a religion built on memory, it seems to me, is deep understanding of the patterns and reasons for those traditions, accompanied by significant experience of the ancient practice. Then, and then only, can it be adapted (and occasionally rejected) in modern settings and fresh expressions. New church and worship leaders need to engage in double listening—to the people among whom they live and to the inheritance of the church of God.

My emphasis on listening to and learning from the tradition needs a counterbalance. We also listen to the cries of the people, which become the 'stuff', the raw material of worship. It is astonishing to see, in many inherited church contexts, how a vapid obsession with the 'set texts' means that those who lead the people gloss over or miss entirely the individual pains and joys that are brought to church Sunday by Sunday. The wise leader will also spiritually and psychologically intuit the 'spiritual mood' of the congregation and weave it into the prayers, praise and confession of the people. We can never be sure, therefore, what the act of worship will turn into. Such an approach is far more exhausting than leading an act of worship by rote, but far more honest and satisfying, too.

Then, too, we are required to listen to what God is saying. This is not a charismatic extra. The fact that we are a people of the word demands of us attention to that word, and this gift of discernment must be used by the whole community. Contemporary lively Christianity has many attractive features, but one of its major weaknesses is the professionalisation not only of the musical tradition but of the whole leadership team. Only those 'sitting on the stage' know the mind of God. It is ironic that those who most strongly criticise the old tradition of the omnicompetent priest are in danger of reinventing it and marginalising those who may equally well discern the voice of God: the weak, the young, the old and the 'uneducated'.

Liquid worship with a strong core

There will be considerable fluidity, experimentation and change. Failures will not be uncommon. There will be much bumpiness, although that won't trouble a people who trust each other and are exploring what it might mean to love God. (A bunch of flowers given to a potential lover who—we discover—has bad hay fever may be embarrassing and a bit of a setback, but no disaster.)

Underpinning that liquidity and uncertainty will be certain emerging patterns, based on scriptural principles, the polarities of human experience and culturally appropriate ritual language. My reading of the history of Christian worship, coupled with a lot of years in a variety of churches, leads me to believe that there is a deep core which will almost always surface when our pioneering explorations are faithful to the gospel and the people among whom we live and move and have our being. This core will include worship elements of:

- meal hospitality and Communion
- opportunities to do, to touch, to taste, to smell, as well as to hear and see, a sensory, fleshy (not fleshly!), engaged worship, fully sacramental

- storytelling in thanksgiving and confession, and out of need, which will turn into a range of types of prayer
- what John Wimber called 'power ministry', an approach to worship that expects the unexpected: a God who frequently intervenes or interrupts proceedings, a God who touches and changes people
- the 'reading' of scripture (placed in inverted commas because one of our current problems is that we assume that scripture must always be declaimed). The truth is that there are myriad ways in which people may 'receive' and teach one another the word of God.

In summary, worship will include a Word–Sacrament–Spirit continuum that signifies the whole of the revelation of the glory of God.

Holy God, holy worship

Additionally, there is a general 'ethos' of Christian worship that regularly cries out for drama, music and an aesthetic sense. God is the author and creator of all that is good and true and beautiful. Proper Christian worship will always proclaim truth, speak of the values of God and reflect the beauty that arises from the character of God and is imprinted on his world. This, not a dull and imprisoned moralism, speaks of the holy God of Revelation 4.

This plea must not be interpreted as a call for perfection. It may be the beauty of the laugh of a young child, the testimony of an old man who has met God face-to-face, the tears of someone who finds herself accepted for the first time in her life, or the offertory dance of a group of visiting African Christians. A football match watched on Sunday morning together in the church hall, the holding of a dying person's hand, or a wine-tasting—all partake of the beauty of God.

Accompanying this dramatic ethos is a focus on transformation: if worship is all that we are, delighting in all that God is, and a genuine encounter takes place, individuals will be challenged from time to time to surrender themselves more fully to a life hidden with Christ in God. This is the work of the Holy Spirit and cannot be programmed into the equation. Opportunities for such response can, however, be built in. When I arrived in England in 1968 as a relatively unthinking Christian, it was members of the Christian Union, asking me if I was born again, who gave me the chance to consider the question. I discovered that I was indeed 'in Christ' but needed to become a 'public Christian', to surrender my inner self to him in the marketplace.

It may be that the age of the 'altar call' is over, although I remain to be persuaded. I have no doubt that we sometimes need to build in to our worship times of challenge and response. Such responses will go well beyond the individualised starting points of faith, to moments of challenge for the whole congregation—calls to holiness.

Mission-shaped worship

There are no final answers, no fixed canon of liturgy. Some people, reading that, will consider such a statement to be an act of extreme unfaithfulness to ordination vows, church constitutions and canons and the heritage of faith in Christendom. So be it. We are in a revolutionary age: the death of Christendom can only be replaced by a gospel of radical obedience that is willing to walk with Christ into new and completely uncertain places.

As we walk, however, we will discover increasingly that there is no place for a condemnation of the old ways. Let the sociologists indulge in assessment; let the dead bury their own dead. The reality is that we are here as Christians today because of the faithfulness and practice of Christians down the ages, not despite them. We do not reject the gospel tradition because it is all bad. We simply interrogate the tradition in the light of new and unprecedented contexts; we reconfigure our responses to a Christ who is 'the same yesterday, today and for ever' (Hebrews 13:8) but who, on earth, tailored his conversation to the people he found at the wells, in the crowds and up trees. We will always be bringing 'out of our treasure things old and things new' (Matthew 13:52) in the laboratory of fragmentary, experimental and emerging worship.

We must never forget that Christian worship draws us into the presence of God, then into his heart and a place of surrender. From there it expels us into the messy world of brokenness, sin, pain, joy, fun and everyday reality. This is not an expulsion from Eden. It is an expulsion with God, whose companions we are, into the place that needs turning into his kingdom on earth. What happens 'in church' must necessarily use the same language and currency as the language of that world, infect it with God and restore its hope. Perhaps the time has come for us to leave the cathedrals of the urban, established, tailored tradition of the Roman Christianity first brought to these islands in the Gregorian mission, and return to the high and holy places of those who came first to these islands— the eccentric individuals and communities whose all-consuming passion for Christ painted mountains and seas, communities and monasteries, books, farms and boats with the glory of God. In so doing, they dispelled the darkness in his name and won the battle in their generation.

A pioneer's story

I am a Church Army evangelist with a background as an artist. Following extensive exploration, Church Army agreed to support a new post in Cornwall. My wife Angela and I relocated to Falmouth in May 2009 with an open brief: 'To engage with artists and others in explorations of faith and spirituality, through art and the Christian contemplative tradition, following God's leading in mission, to seek the creation of a fresh expression of Christian community.' Although we worship at one of the local parish churches, I am not part of any church's staff team. I am licensed by the Bishop of Truro to minister throughout the diocese, which also provides line management support.

On arrival, I felt it was important not to rush into anything but to spend time asking God to reveal who and what to engage with— for the gift of discernment and 'divine appointments'. For this to happen, I needed space. Like many of us, I can easily become busy, filling my days, weeks, months and so on. If there was pressure to do anything, its source was my 'inner critic', laying on the guilt.

I had loads of questions. How was I to meet artists and art lovers? Once I'd met some, how would explorations of faith begin? I sensed that God was saying, 'Colin, don't try too hard. Let go, and let me arrange things.' There seems to be an ease to the way the answers are slowly coming. It feels like an unfolding of the way to go—like a bolt of cloth being opened out.

I don't always sense God's hand or presence, but I have a deep peace about his grace at work in the world. It's one thing to say that 'mission is finding out what God's doing...' but how do I find that out? In part, the answer comes through trusting my own gut instincts, including those times when it feels important to say 'No' or 'Wait'. Gradually, 'people of peace' have come along (see Luke 10:6), surprises have happened and opportunities have presented themselves. In this past year, I have felt more at ease about how to do mission and evangelism than ever before. One of the hardest things is letting go of my baggage. I carry so much: ways of thinking about how to do mission, worship and church. I sense God's invitation to be open to completely new things, but can I take the risk of waiting, of not doing the next best idea that comes along in my head, or through otther people's suggestions?

I am finding that some people get it, others are bemused, and some don't understand at all, and I am often surprised by who is included in each of those categories. Those who do get it include many from outside the church, and there are many inside who don't understand at all. I have had to be clear that the focus of my work is outside the church, so that those within it (leaders and congregations) can give me the freedom not to be in it too much. I made sure that I communicated this clearly at an early stage. I also emphasised that I wouldn't be bringing people back into their churches, but valued their support and prayers in my endeavour to develop something new. I seek to encourage a sense of partnership with local church.

As I have said, I wondered how to gather people to 'engage with artists and others in explorations of faith and spirituality, through art...' I had to wait for a while, but, when the answer came, it came as a gift and from an unexpected source. Tate St Ives Gallery has piloted a project throughout Cornwall called 'Look Groups'. They are like book groups, but the focus is art. Through joining an evening art class, I was put forward to facilitate the Falmouth group, where our discussions cover many aspects of art, including spirituality and faith. It feels as though the space given to waiting and not rushing is being honoured through opportunities and

....

connecting with 'people of peace'.

A major aspect of my work is for me to paint. My prayer is that my paintings reflect my faith and convey something of the gospel as people from outside the church see them exhibited. It feels important to be doing this—being an artist among the artists I feel called to work with. I want to be able to relate to them, to understand something of their issues and lives. However, spending time 'just painting' also feels too good to be true! 'Is this work?' I ask myself. Yet, if my gift was preaching or teaching or writing, the church would welcome my sermon or teaching tour, or my latest book. In this visual age, why not use art as a means of communicating the gospel? It often feels as if I have to give myself permission to do it. I wonder if this is because of the way we do church, and my past experience of what it means to be in ministry.

I was invited to be part of the chaplaincy team at the local art college, which is one of the largest in the UK. Initially I struggled with the role and wasn't sure how to engage the students and staff. I felt I had to learn new ways of ministry as I simply came alongside people. I wanted to offer an Art and Spirituality seminar but felt unsure about being seen as some kind of expert. In the end (with encouragement from the chaplain), I went for it. The result is a regular discussion group with artists who want to explore links between their own art and the spiritual, as well as learning from others.

My hope and prayer is that all this bears much fruit for the kingdom of God. At this point, I do not know how long that might take, and what 'fruit' might look like. I know that God has called and equipped me for the task, however, and I trust that whatever the results will be, he asks me to be faithful rather than successful.

Colin Brown is a Church Army Creative Arts Evangelist based in Falmouth, Cornwall.

....

9

In for the long haul? Sustaining fresh expressions of church

Mike Moynagh

The question of how to sustain fresh expressions of church is shooting up the agenda as growing numbers of them are brought to birth. Sceptics wonder if these new forms of church are durable; dioceses and denominations seek to invest in ventures that will last, while practitioners ask how they can keep their new churches fresh and fruitful. Sustaining fresh expressions raises a galaxy of questions about discipleship, worship, relationships to the wider church and much else. This chapter picks up just some of the issues.

What do we mean by sustainability?

Often, sustainability is understood in terms of the 'three selfs',[1] which were formulated separately by the 19th-century missionary strategists, Henry Venn and Rufus Anderson. The three 'selfs' refer to missionary ventures that become self-financing, self-governing and self-reproducing (or self-propagating). Some people add a fourth 'self': self-theologising.[2] A sustainable venture will develop a 'local theology' that responds to its context.

Is the 'three selfs' approach still valid?

Applying this model of sustainability to fresh expressions has much to commend it. The assumption that ventures should stand on their own feet takes seriously people's need for appropriate autonomy if they are to flourish. Communities, as much as individuals, need proper space if they are to reach their potential.

Experience suggests, however, that this model reflects the patterns of inherited church too strongly to be applicable in all cases. It assumes that all fresh expressions will be like church plants in the past, such as 'daughter' churches that eventually became independent. Many fresh expressions, even those based on a local church, are not like that (although some are). For example, youth congregations are unlikely to be financially independent. Other initiatives will continue to share their parent church's administrative arrangements and be part of its governance structure, such as a church emerging within an older people's luncheon club.

The model is also too static for some fresh expressions, a number of which last only for a season. A church in a leisure centre or workplace may come to an end when a key member moves to another part of the country. A Christian gathering on a campus may dissolve when the students graduate. A mid-sized community with a missional focus may run out of energy. In the 'benefits culture', membership and attendance may be so fluid that the venture always feels fragile.

In particular, the focus on 'self' downplays interdependence. The 'three selfs principle' was developed to hasten the formation of churches that could stand on their own feet, without their mission-ary founders. It was designed to encourage missionaries to move on, and the stress was on independence, to counter dependence. Applied today, however, this emphasis comes at a cost. Independence can be seen as a virtue, while interdependence, expressed through local church, denominational or ecumenical ties, goes unmentioned. Surely mutual dependence is more God-like, and in keeping with church as fellowship, than heroic independence?

Perhaps we should understand sustainability in a more flexible and fluid way. So we might expect a fresh expression to be:

- *connected to the wider church* in relationships of mutual respect and support. This will enable the fresh expression to help sustain the whole body, as well as allowing the wider body to be a source of sustenance for the fresh expression.
- *appropriately independent*. The degree of financial, administrative and other independence will vary from one context to another.
- *viable for its lifespan*. Some new churches will be seasonal, others longer-term. The accent should be on viability while the community lasts, rather than always on the goal of permanence.
- *attentive to flow*. Fresh expressions will manage the flow of their members to other Christian communities so that individuals have a sustained church involvement. If members of a teenage congregation go away to college, they will be put in touch with Christians in the places to which they move. If a venture comes to the end of its natural life, members will receive aid in finding an alternative community. If individuals need to change church as their spirituality evolves or circumstances change, they will be helped to do so. In some contexts, sustainability will be more about flow than about durability.

It will be important not to fill in these details too early, to avoid prejudging what the fresh expression will be like. The meaning of 'appropriate independence', for example, may become apparent only as the emerging church develops. It is crucial not to close down possibilities by prejudging how the Spirit will lead.

Identifying fruitfulness

Having a clear understanding of what is meant by fruitfulness—and being able to measure it—is an important aspect of understanding sustainability. Some Christians find the idea of measurement difficult because they want to avoid anything that smacks of the target culture. But assessing fruitfulness is a means of discerning where and how the Spirit is at work. It allows us to ask the question (as should also be asked of an inherited church): is our fresh expression a fruitful or barren branch of the vine (John 15:1–8)?

If church is what happens when people encounter the risen Lord, as Archbishop Rowan Williams suggests, and if signs of this encounter are growth in a gathering's UP, IN, OUT and OF relationships,[3] then we have some criteria for discerning fruitfulness.

Are members of the fresh expression growing:

- UP in their relationships with God?
- IN in their relationships together?
- OUT in their relationships of service to the world?
- in the OF relationship to the wider church?

Growth in these relationships will look different in different settings, and the various traditions of the church will understand the relationships in different ways, so 'UP, IN, OUT, OF' is not a mechanical formula for identifying fruitfulness. Nor should these criteria be expressed through targets that are imposed on a fresh expression by an outside body. Rather, they are a framework within which conversations about fruitfulness can occur.

These conversations may include interpretations of numbers (such as 'How many people are we reaching?') but they will also be likely to include an evaluation of 'soft' data. The latter might be collected, for instance, through focus groups, informal conversations with people in the community ('What impact do you think we are having?') or feedback sessions within the gathering ('How are we getting on?')[4]

What information is collected and how it is collected will vary from context to context, but using it prayerfully will help a fresh expression to discern what the Spirit has been doing and what issues in its life it may be called to address.

Sustaining the pioneer

Whatever the size of venture, it is easy for leaders to get burnt out and put the church-start at risk. Many will also be new to the task and so will need to learn as they go along. To a significant extent, the health of the Christian community will be bound up with the well-being of its leaders.

Selecting the right people is an obvious first step in sustaining pioneers. Typically, pioneers should be gatherers of people, have sufficient leadership gifts for the size of the venture, have the right cultural fit and have robust spiritual lives. Attending to their walk with God will be pioneers' first responsibility.

Appropriate support should be available. Depending on the scale and type of venture, the pioneer will need:

- someone to cry and laugh with
- a spiritual director/companion
- prayer support
- appropriate training—for example, in the theology and practice of fresh expressions
- a coach or mentor who can not only listen but also advise and warn (but not judge), perhaps saying, 'Others have done this…' or, 'Are you sure you're not going down the wrong track?'
- advice from others in a similar field, preferably from someone who has planted a fresh expression in a similar context or been involved in a comparable type of venture
- peer support—meeting up with others leading fresh expressions
- specialist expertise in finance, legal and other matters.[5]

This is a lot of support to ask for, although some of the sources may overlap. That should not be surprising. We live in an ever more sophisticated world, in which complex tasks are mushrooming. Leading a fresh expression, even a simple one, requires a considerable degree of skill.

It is usually best for pioneers to be encouraged to make their own arrangements for support: it then becomes their support. But if a church or group of churches is appointing a pioneer (for example, on a new housing estate), it may want to take responsibility for providing some of this support initially, until the pioneer has found their feet.

Laying the right foundations

Fresh expressions emerge organically and often in unexpected ways, but their final shape is frequently determined by the DNA that is implanted in the early stages. The direction in which they start tends to determine where they end up. So, if a pioneer gathers a core team of disaffected church leavers, it will be no great surprise if the church that emerges is full of similar people. There need be nothing wrong with that, unless the pioneer felt passionately called to reach a different segment of the population. Likewise, if individuals gather round an agenda in which there is no hint that a Christian dimension will be explicit, introducing that element later may be difficult: 'We didn't sign up to that!' people will say.

This means that it is helpful to think carefully, early on, about the key values that God may be calling the fresh expression to reflect, including values to do with sustainability. Becoming sustainable begins with the intention to be sustainable. If you hope your fresh expression will 'self-reproduce', for example, you may want to consider how this intention will be communicated to those who join the community and how it will be kept at the front of their minds. What part will this expectation play in the way individuals are introduced to the faith? If you expect your fresh expression to exist only for a season, what will you do from an early stage to make it easy for members to join another gathering?

Questions to do with governance—how the fresh expression

sits within a denomination, for instance—may be best answered when it is clear what sort of community the Spirit has brought to birth. But agreeing early on how this and other such issues will be addressed, by whom and when, may prevent misunderstandings from arising later.

Size to fit the context

From the earliest days, midwives of church should ask, 'What sort of venture would be sustainable in this context?' Being contextual about size is especially vital in relation to financial sustainability. What sort of financial commitment will be sustainable by the people whom the initiative is called to serve?

The answer may warn the founding team against a venture that requires considerable outside financial support to get off the ground. Such support may be available from charitable trusts or public bodies, but it will almost certainly be of limited duration. What will happen when the money runs out? Will there be sufficient resources from within the community to keep the new church going?

Being thoroughly realistic may discourage teams from starting over-elaborate projects that can't be sustained in the long term and will produce heartache and disappointment when they eventually fold.

Of course, this presents an ethical dilemma. If church-starts in poor areas always accommodate themselves to what the local people can afford, the spread of income will remain stubbornly unequal: outside grants help in only a small way to redistribute wealth. Against this must be set the advantages of starting on a sustainable basis and scaling up step-by-step once each new stage becomes financially self-sustaining. There are no easy answers, but it may help in the early days to ask questions like:

- What are the financial resources of the people we are called to serve?
- What sized initiative could they realistically sustain?
- For how long will the initial funding last?
- Is replacement funding from outside likely?
- Are we thinking on too large a scale?

'Simple church' may be a helpful concept in relation to all this. A simple church might comprise, for example, a weekly or fortnightly gathering round a bring-and-share meal. The latest film or the ethical dimensions of a news story might form the basis of the conversation.

One meal-based church among students in Paris started with the hors d'oeuvre, during which people caught up with each other. There was a short talk on a subject like forgiveness, which was discussed over the main course. Topics for prayer were collected over the dessert, and after prayer people had coffee.

The convenor's hope was that modelling something so simple would encourage students to start similar communities when they moved away. Simple churches, with their limited demands on leadership, may be easier to reproduce than complex ones. Is this, perhaps, one reason why the New Testament household churches put down roots and multiplied? Simple church also suits contexts where resources are scarce, and it can fit easily into time-squeezed lives: it doesn't need a great deal of time-consuming organisation. It works with the grain of our busy, busy culture.

Simple church does have limitations, though. Especially if numbers are small and the convenor is untrained, the range of input may be limited. New believers may be fed on quite a restricted spiritual diet. Online and other published resources can help, of course, but the spiritual life of emerging Christians will be further enriched if they have the opportunity to meet with larger groups of believers.

It may be that two or three small groups can 'cluster' together every few weeks to provide this wider experience.[6] Alternatively, or in addition, a small group might periodically worship with a bigger congregation nearby (such as its parent church, if it has one), take part in townwide Christian events or attend a Christian festival such as Greenbelt or the Walsingham Pilgrimage.

Forming 'coalitions of the willing' among local churches (both fresh expressions and inherited), to pool resources for mission and discipleship, is an urgent priority for theological and practical reasons. In particular, local collaboration would help simple churches to avoid being isolated. It should feature strongly in discussions about sustainability. Might 'simple' and 'connected' be good words to keep together?

Transition from first- to second-generation leaders

The crucial process of passing on leadership starts with the right mindset: not 'This is a project for other people' but 'This is a project with...'. When we build on that foundation, it raises questions about when and how the transition of leadership should be done.

When should the transition occur?

About a century ago, Roland Allen, who served as a missionary in North China, argued that missionaries should allow their converts to stand on their own feet as soon as possible. Should this be a principle for fresh expressions?

Allen used the apostle Paul as his model. He pointed out that Paul rarely stayed with his new congregations for more than six months. Missionaries, he claimed, should move on rapidly in a similar way. They should rely not on their continued presence to guide believers into a mature Christian life, but on scripture and the Holy Spirit.[7]

Can this principle be applied to contemporary pioneering? Caution is advisable. Allen seems to have read Paul through rose-tinted spectacles. Time and again, Paul left his new churches quickly because of local opposition rather than through choice (see, for example, Acts 13:50; 14:5–6, 20; 17:5–10, 13–14). Indeed, after being driven out of Thessalonica, Paul became highly anxious about the fate of his fledgling church there (1 Thessalonians 2:17—3:5). He seems to have worried that he had had to leave too soon. In Corinth and Ephesus, where he had greater freedom, he stayed for over 18 months and three years respectively.[8] Leaving new churches quickly does not seem to have been Paul's intentional strategy.

Moreover, at the core of these churches appear to have been converts from the local synagogue, where Paul typically started his missionary work (Acts 14:1). These Jews and 'God-fearing Gentiles' were already monotheists rather than believers in several gods, and at least some, it seems, knew their scriptures (our Old Testament) well (17:11). Appointing elders from among them may not have been as much of a challenge as it is in some circumstances today, when new believers may have virtually no biblical knowledge.

Jesus does provide an alternative model. His departure at the ascension left the disciples humanly responsible for the formation and expansion of the Church. Jesus intentionally delegated his leadership, and those assuming responsibility were far from being the finished spiritual article. Matthew tells us that some of the eleven disciples (it could read 'many') still doubted (28:17). Yet Jesus did not allow these doubts to derail his delegation. Rather, he embedded the principle of handing over leadership into the very origins of the Church.

However, unlike Paul (according to Allen's account), Jesus did not exit after only a few months. His closest disciples spent some three years with him, day after day. This was mentoring of a highly intense kind. Then, after the resurrection came further teaching about the kingdom of God (Acts 1:3). The followers of Jesus needed prolonged teaching and deep immersion in the practice of discipleship before they could be entrusted with the Church. The model is one of allowing new believers to be well formed spiritually before the leader moves on.

Might we learn from both Jesus and Paul? If Jesus' model emphasises the importance of proper formation before passing on leadership, Paul's experience (despite being often driven by necessity) suggests that in some situations the handover can be remarkably fast. The two pictures qualify each other. Paul's warns against raising the bar of Christian maturity too high before handing over leadership. Jesus' warns against being too optimistic about the time it will take church founders to accomplish their initial discipling task. The timing of when to move on clearly requires discernment in context.

What criteria might we use to discern when to make the transition? Both Jesus and Paul left their new churches with the Holy Spirit, a basic understanding of the gospel, scripture (our Old Testament), the sacraments of baptism and Holy Communion, leadership (Jesus left the apostles; Paul left elders: Acts 14:23) and, in the case of Paul, ongoing human support. Paul revisited his new churches when he could (see, for example, Acts 14:21), sent members of his team to sort out problems (2 Corinthians 7:13; 8:16–22) and wrote pastoral letters. Might this provide a framework to help pioneers decide when to hand over their leadership?

Preparing for the transition

If we take seriously the principle of handing on leadership, it will affect every aspect of a fresh expression's life. It will shape the basic strategy. It is striking that Paul set up house churches: this was not necessarily the obvious thing to do. The synagogue, which had been so central to Paul's life, offered an alternative model. As the number of Jewish (and Gentile) worshippers grew, a central building for the purpose of worship was established.

Yet Paul did not follow this example. Instead, he encouraged house churches to proliferate. Was this because small units, based on the home where a head of the household already existed, made the indigenisation of leadership more straightforward? As key heads of families converted, they became church leaders in their own homes.[9]

If this was Paul's intention (though we are not told whether it was or not), what would be the equivalents today? What would it mean for a contextual church planting strategy to be built partly around the leadership requirements of the envisaged churches? What would these communities look like?

Indigenising leadership will influence the way individuals are encouraged into the faith. Will the process foster dependence on the pioneer, making it more difficult for the latter to leave? Or will it model reliance on the Holy Spirit and the resources of the community? Will the pioneer act as an expert or a facilitator?

A pioneer convening a 'spirituality at work' group, for instance, might buy a book of Christian meditations, lead the first couple of sessions from the book and then pass the book to others in the group to lead subsequent sessions. This group would be weaned from the pioneer's leadership at an early stage.

The core team/community might periodically consider not just this, but every aspect of the emerging church's life. How far is leadership being shared? Are models being used that foster dependency?

Issues to keep in mind

Special sensitivity may be needed among people within the 'benefits culture'. They are so used to outsiders coming into the area from secular agencies, advancing their own careers and then leaving, that to see the pattern repeated in the church could leave them disillusioned. The sudden departure of someone who has brought them together into a community, however fluid and chaotic, may be profoundly painful and may confirm their cynicism. So the transition to second-generation leadership must be handled with particular care in this context.

One ordained pioneer in this type of area sought to manage the transition by withdrawing gradually. She shared more and more tasks with others in her team and continued to make herself available to the person who replaced her as leader. In contrast to her predecessor, who had left the year before and avoided further contact, she stayed in touch with members of the community. People felt less abandoned.

Continuing links with the pioneer who has left can make practical sense. If serious problems arise, usually the founder of the community will be better placed than others to help sort them out. He or she will already have the relationships and the authority required.

Encouraging a continuing link with the founder would follow the practice of Paul, who had to intervene in some of his new churches either through correspondence or by sending emissaries, like Timothy (1 Corinthians 4:17). Yet such intervention today will often be problematic because a pioneer's authority is normally expected to cease when they move away: the community comes under someone else's authority. This situation can be far from ideal. The new leader may not have had time to build the required relationships of trust before major difficulties in the fresh expression occur, and may not be as well placed as the founder to facilitate a resolution.

Is this an example of how some traditional arrangements jar with what could work best in a fresh expressions context? As 'serial pioneers' emerge and establish a network of fresh expressions, how will their authority in the network square with the denominational authorities?

Other issues might include the ordination of leaders: professional clergy, arguably, are more inclined than lay people to breed spiritual dependency. They may see themselves as 'experts', which will make indigenising leadership more difficult. Although this is not the only consideration, might it be an argument for lay-led fresh expressions?

A leader with a strong, charismatic personality is more likely to create dependency than a leader who is lower-key, again making the transition to new leadership harder. This may raise questions about deployment. Might charismatic leaders sometimes be more effectively engaged in recruiting, equipping and leading teams of church founders who multiply fresh expressions, rather than heading up a single venture?

Risk is always the big worry. Pioneers and others, understandably, fear that things may go wrong if the pioneer leaves too early. But that was the same problem that Paul faced—and things did go wrong. Think of the church in Corinth! Leadership involves learning by experience, including by making mistakes. Mistakes are the price of allowing new Christians to grow in their leadership gifts. It is a real price, but the gain is greater maturity and human flourishing.

What about pioneers who want to settle?

Having started a church, some founders feel called to settle within it and lead it to the next phase. This might seem to be at odds with the model of leaving. However, settling may be appropriate on some occasions, especially where the founder is leading a church plant into reproduction, or where a small Christian community has formed round a person's passion or among their network of friends. The community is so much part of the founder's life that withdrawing from it would not make sense.

In these cases, much will depend on the settler's style of leadership. A releasing style will enable leadership gifts to flourish within the community and, at its best, will encourage individuals to initiate their own fresh expressions in the contexts where they live and work. The danger, of course, is that settling can mask the desire to retain control, which then impedes the expression of gifts and makes it harder for the community to realise its potential.

Managing other transitions

Like most organisations, as a fresh expression starts and grows, there will be times when it faces the challenge of making a significant transition. Sometimes the transition will be a matter of survival: the volunteer manager on which a café church depends moves out of the area, for example, or the parent church withdraws funding. At other times the transition will involve growth, such as a cell-based expression of church expanding to two cells or a church plant starting a second plant.

In these situations, the venture has to transition to a new phase either to survive or to grow. Successfully making these transitions is an important part of sustainability. They enable the community to remain fruitful or become more so.

One simple secular model, taken from the many volumes that have been written about managing change in organisations, suggests that in navigating transitions, the key task for leaders is to help the organisation:

- *to start with values.* What are we about? What do we want to achieve? These questions get back to fundamentals and ensure a focus on the wood rather than the trees.
- *to agree the principles that will guide how these values are expressed.* A cell-based church intending to grow further cells might agree four principles: each cell will have a mission focus, they will meet at least three times a month, their leaders will meet regularly in an accountability group, and the cells will cluster together once a month.
- *to allow maximum flexibility within these principles.* This freedom permits individuals to be creative within a framework that serves the organisation's purpose. Energy is released and fresh thinking about how to make the transition results.[10]

Such an approach gives expression to Paul's vision of shared ministry within the body (Romans 12; 1 Corinthians 12) and reflects something of the way that Christ exercises servant leadership within the kingdom.

Keeping fresh

There is a well-known process by which organisations become institutionalised. A magnetic leader with an inspirational vision forms a community, which stabilises in the second generation and formalises criteria for membership. In subsequent generations, much of the energy goes into maintaining and protecting established structures to ensure the community continues. Can fresh expressions avoid following this pattern?

John Drane has argued that there are tendencies that threaten to suck life out of the fresh expressions movement (if it can be called that).[11] As part of a 'McDonaldisation' process, he lists:

- the concern for efficiency, such as succumbing to the temptation to replicate a model that has worked elsewhere.
- a trend toward calculability, as demands grow to see numerical results.
- a desire for predictability—conformity to some pattern or other.
- a desire to retain some form of control in existing churches.

He suggests four values that can work in the opposite direction:

- creativity as opposed to efficiency.
- relationality instead of calculability.
- flexibility (or adaptability) rather than predictability.
- proactivity—straining forward instead of holding on to the past—in place of control.

However, John Drane does not explain how these four counter-values can become the heartbeat of an emerging church. To understand this, self-organising (or complexity) theory can make a contribution.

An example of the fruits of self-organising theory is the three-point process described above: start with the values, agree the principles that will guide how these values are expressed, and allow maximum flexibility within these principles. Regular reviews by the core team/community can bring this self-organising process into a fresh expression on an ongoing basis, rather than merely as part of transition management. For instance, values and principles can be regularly reviewed, involving others in the community. Questions can be asked as to whether there is enough flexibility.

The flexibility given by making this process continuous will encourage creativity, the participation involved will promote relationality, and the regular reviews of values and principles will foster proactivity. Participation and constant small changes will be the likely result. The conclusions of one study of business entrepreneurs illustrate how participation, coupled with continuous small change, can keep an organisation fresh:

Testing new ideas is an important way of preventing institutionalisation, something that both the Visionary entrepreneurs [who were interviewed] do. One of them says, 'We always test all proposals [on the rest of the staff] and we don't see anything as stupid.' This brings flexibility into the process and prevents habits. An important part in the dynamic process is to make small changes regularly and this develops the business.[12]

Being creative and flexible may mean bringing seasonality into the heart of a fresh expression: activities are undertaken only for a period. The pattern of worship might be changed regularly. Communities with a missional focus might have a limited life. A youth congregation might last for a time, before giving way to a differently shaped gathering. If constant flux within a fresh expression feels too unsettling ('We'll do this for a while, then something else, then something else again'), it may be helpful to remember that seasonality can be for a season too. In other words, 'We've had a season of constant change, now let us have a season of stability before we allow God to lead us into another season of change.'

Conclusion

This brings us back to the beginning. Contemporary society is marked by flow and fluidity, as work becomes increasingly mobile (moving, for an individual, from the office to the train and to the hotel in a day), as friends use their mobile phones to fix and change meetings at the last minute, and as consumers (despite the recession) migrate from one product to the next. But within this movement, there are sizable islands of stability. Before the recession, for example, UK homeowners remained in their homes for an average of 15 years, and the trend to stay put had been stable. When people did move, 60 per cent stayed within a five-mile radius of their previous property.[13] For the most part, family ties remain close. In 2001, just over half of adults living separately from their parents saw their mother weekly, the same proportion as six years earlier.[14]

In a society combining flux and stability, we should not be surprised if the emerging 'mixed economy' of church contains these two dimensions as well. Some fresh expressions will be seasonal, others durable. The concept of sustainability needs room for both.

Notes

1 For example, *Mission-Shaped Church* (CHP, 2004), pp. 120–123.

2 Although it does not usually use the term 'self-theologising', this is one of the thrusts of the post-Vatican II writing on contextual theology. A key text is Robert J. Schreiter, *Constructing Local Theologies* (SCM, 1985).

3 *Mission-Shaped Church*, pp. vii, 98–99.

4 Charities often use quite sophisticated tools to evaluate softer outcomes (see, for example, www.homelessoutcomes.org.uk), and these might be adapted in some cases.

5 For an alternative list, with much overlap, see Juliet Kilpin and Stuart Murray, *Church Planting in the Inner City: The urban expression story* (Grove, 2007), p. 26.

6 For a discussion of this, see Bob Hopkins and Mike Breen, *Clusters: Creative mid-sized missional communities* (3dm Publications, 2007).

7 See, for example, Roland Allen, *Missionary Methods: St Paul's or Ours?* (Lutterworth, 2006), chs. 8, 9, 10.

8 Eckhard J. Schnabel, *Paul the Missionary: Realities, strategies and methods* (IVP, 2008), pp. 104, 108.

9 Roger Gehring argues that Paul intentionally recruited householders, whose homes would act as a base for local and regional mission. Roger W. Gehring, *House Church and Mission: The importance of household structures in early Christianity* (Hendrickson, 2004), pp. 185–187.

10 This is based on Benyamin Bergmann Litchenstein, 'Self-organized transitions: a pattern amid the chaos of transformative change', *The Academy of Management Executive* (1993–2005), 14 (4), 2000, pp. 128–141. It should go without saying that caution is needed when applying research findings from the business world to the church.

11 John Drane, 'Resisting McDonaldization: Fresh Expressions of church for a new millennium' in Viggo Mortensen and Andreas Osterlund Nielsen (eds.), *Walk Humbly with the Lord: Church and mission engaging plurality* (Eerdmans, 2011).

12 Ingmari Cantzler and Svante Leijon, 'Team-oriented women entrepreneurs: a way to modern management', *Journal of Small Business and Enterprise Development*, 14 (4), 2007, pp. 743–744.

13 'A moving experience: How often do people move home and mortgages?', *CML Market Briefing Special Article* (April 2004).

14 Alison Park and Ceridwen Roberts, 'The ties that bind' in Alison Park et al. (eds.), *British Social Attitudes: The 19th Report* (Sage, 2002), p. 203.

10

From one pioneer to another: insights from St Paul

John Drane

Much recent thinking about fresh expressions and pioneer ministry has focused on a rediscovery of the importance of following Jesus' example in the missionary task that now faces us in a post-Christian culture. At an early stage in the journey, Archbishop Rowan Williams set the tone in his foreword to the *Mission-Shaped Church* report, with his insistence that 'church is what happens when people encounter the Risen Jesus and commit themselves to sustaining and deepening that encounter in their encounter with each other'.[1] More recently, reflecting on his time as leader of Fresh Expressions, Bishop Steven Croft emphasised the need for Christians above all to be 'Jesus' people',[2] and some are insistent that an authentically missional church will place a higher value on Christology than on inherited ecclesiologies, of whatever tradition or persuasion.[3]

While that suggestion raises its own questions—not least because our knowledge about Jesus, even in the New Testament Gospels, has always been mediated through the church—it would be hard to fault this renewed emphasis on Jesus as the 'pioneer and perfecter of our faith' (Hebrews 12:2). In many respects it can be viewed as a healthy corrective to much inherited thinking about the nature of the church, which, insofar as it has drawn on biblical themes, has tended to give pride of place to the teachings of Paul on the matter. Previous generations were inclined to justify that emphasis by questioning whether Jesus ever intended to found any sort of community (whether or not it might be designated as a 'church'), and frequently dismissed the isolated use of the word ekklesia in the Jesus tradition as a later attempt to find dominical warrant for something that was inherently alien to the core message of the kingdom as taught by Jesus.

Most commentators today would regard such a distinction between kingdom and church as, at best, an exaggeration. But many still feel much happier with Jesus than they do with Paul, even though a straightforward reading of the New Testament suggests that Paul was one of the most successful missional pioneers of the first century, from whom we might imagine we could learn something for our situation today. It is not difficult to understand the reasons for such hesitation, as, depending on who you ask, he was either a hero or a villain. Some see him as an arch-conservative, responsible for defending slavery and misogyny, not to mention his alleged anti-Semitic and homophobic tendencies, while others describe him as 'remarkably faithful to the message and vision of Jesus himself... a faithful apostle of the radical Jesus'.[4]

There can be no doubt that, for much of his life, Paul was at the centre of acrimonious debates and disagreements not only about his own relationship to Judaism but regarding his understanding of the Hebrew scriptures and of the relationship of God's ancient covenants to the new covenant in Christ. These debates, in one form or another, still continue as scholars argue about the appropriate frame of reference within which his theology can be understood.[5] It is therefore hardly surprising that, if missional practitioners think of Paul at all, they tend to dismiss him as a peddler of somewhat arcane ideas that are not going to be central to the task now facing us.[6]

Arguably, this is just one manifestation of a much bigger question facing missional pioneers today, many of whom are either embarrassed to use the Bible or have no idea how to do it in ways that will have integrity with their own situation as well as with the original setting of its various books. An inherited paradigm that sees scripture first and foremost as a way of addressing analytical, propositional questions tends to regard practical missional questions as irrelevant, or at least beyond its purview. This is not entirely the fault of mission-minded activists, as there is a growing consensus of scholarly opinion that would agree with Walter Wink's depiction of the prevailing historical critical approach to the Bible as 'bankrupt... incapable of achieving what most of its practitioners considered its purpose to be: so to interpret the Scriptures that the past becomes alive and illumines our present with new possibilities for personal and social transformation'.[7]

To unpack the implications of that opinion in relation to the practice of ministry today would require much more than just a single article—a whole book, in fact. But in this, as in other matters, discernment is going to be the key gift of the Spirit for today's pioneers, and identifying the right questions to bring to the Bible will be a central aspect of their discernment. So what are the right questions for pioneers to bring to the apostle Paul? There will be many equally valid answers, but the question I want to ask of him here is a simple one: how can we communicate the good news of Jesus in a way that will be culturally appropriate in the 21st century while remaining faithful to the example of Jesus himself? To engage with that sort of missional question, we need to ask Paul questions about attitude, communication, style and personality. Put another way, what exactly made him tick?

Introducing Paul

Borg and Crossan speak of the need for us to be 'meeting Paul again for the first time',[8] and, when we lay aside our inherited preconceptions about him, some surprising insights emerge. There are some things that Christians tend to take for granted simply because, from our vantage point, we can see the big picture. For example, if the members of most traditional churches were asked what they know about Paul, a significant majority would probably identify him first of all as a letter writer—and many of them would empathise with the writer of 2 Peter, who said, 'There are some things in them hard to understand' (2 Peter 3:16, NRSV). Others would note that, if we want to compile anything that might resemble a life of Paul, then the book of Acts (while not exclusively about him, and raising hermeneutical questions of its own) is the best source we have, and most accounts of his ministry take that as their starting point. Luke's purpose in writing Acts was not, of course, biographical but was related to his own interest in plotting the spread of the faith from Galilee to Rome. In the process of doing so, he wanted to offer examples of contextualised mission that would show how the gospel might be presented in circumstances as diverse as the Jewish synagogue, where the discourse would focus on the Hebrew scriptures and their meaning, and the Athenian Areopagus, with its congregants who 'would spend their time in nothing but telling or hearing something new' (Acts 17:21).

Given our reliance on Acts to provide some sort of chronological framework for the life of Paul, it might come as a surprise to be reminded that Luke (who was himself a personal associate of Paul) makes no reference at all to the writing of letters. If his account of Paul's activities was our only source of knowledge about him, nobody would ever have guessed that he was such a prolific writer. That in itself offers an interesting comment on Paul's approach to mission work. The ancient world had no shortage of gifted indivi-duals, predominantly politicians and philosophers, who spread their message through the medium of the written word. Some of them did so through the use of the literary epistle—documents that looked like letters but were not addressed to any specific readers and fulfilled a role more like a newspaper editorial or a campaigning pamphlet than a personal communication. Paul clearly had the capacity to have done the same, so presumably his preference for the personal encounter was an important part of his thinking on mission. The gospel was not some disembodied set of beliefs that could be debated in abstract ways: it was about relationships, community and personal interaction—which is why almost all his letters were written to those whom he had already encountered face to face.[9]

At the same time, we must take account of the fact that the stories Luke included in Acts are secondary sources of knowledge when compared with Paul's letters, and, while the two kinds of source are by no means incompatible, the letters undoubtedly offer a more intimate insight into his personality. We find here all the challenges that we are facing in pioneer ministry today, and Paul gives us permission, if we need it, to be open and honest about how we deal with them. Far from being the self-confident character of popular imagination, Paul was deeply aware of his own inadequacy for the task (2 Corinthians 4:7–12), and was often frustrated (Philippians 4:2–3; Philemon) in ways that, on occasion, could boil over into anger (Galatians 3:1–5), all of it fuelled by his own ambition to live up to the glorious possibilities held out by faithful discipleship (1 Corinthians 9:20–23). At the same time, he knew that he was on a journey himself, with much still left to discover (Philippians 3:12–16); in his better moments he could be overwhelmingly generous (1 Corinthians 16:1–4; 2 Corinthians 9:1–5), even gentle (1 Thessalonians 2:9–12). When it all got to him, he was not averse to using surprisingly crude language (Galatians 5:12), and everywhere he was passionate.

In other words, far from being a saint in stained glass, Paul was a fully human person. To misappropriate the words of Eric Bazilian's song, which, through Joan Osborne's album *Relish*, hit the charts in 1995, Paul was 'just a slob like one of us'.[10] I can identify with someone like that and admire them for giving us such an honest insight into their dreams and struggles. Nothing is hidden. There is an important insight here about the sort of people God can use: people like us, who struggle and wrestle with themselves as well as the bigger issues of life, faith, God and discipleship.

Paul and his context

Like the rest of us, Paul's life was shaped by his upbringing and the shared history of his people. In his case, growing up in Tarsus, he lived in a public world that was shaped by Greek philosophy and Roman technology and a domestic environment whose roots lay deep in Jewish history and culture. As a young teen, he was sent to complete his education in Jerusalem and entered a different world again—a land that was as thoroughly Hellenised as any other part of the Roman empire, but with a more ambivalent attitude in which an age-old conflict was still being played out, as the traditional values of Jewish belief struggled to come to terms with the all-pervasive Hellenistic culture that had been imposed by a succession of invaders as far back as the days of Alexander the Great (333–323BC). Engaging with his ancestral faith in this situation raised different questions than he would have been familiar with in Tarsus, with diverse and often incompatible attitudes to the prevailing culture adopted by different groups within Palestinian society. His options are still with us today. The Sadducees embraced the prevailing culture and accommodated their faith and lifestyle to fit, while others rejected it entirely by withdrawing into spiritual and physical isolation (for example, the writers of the Dead Sea Scrolls, possibly Essenes); others were determined to resist by any means at their disposal, including violence (the Zealots).

Paul, whether by deliberate choice or divine coincidence, aligned himself with the Pharisees, a group whom modern Christians have often seen as the antithesis of everything the gospel stands for, but who were, in reality, neither as smug nor as hypocritical as they can be made to seem. Rather than either embracing or rejecting the culture, they engaged with it in a way that today would be regarded as contextual mission. Their influence was out of all proportion to their actual numbers (according to contemporary sources, there were only about 6000 of them at the time of Jesus), and one reason for that was the fact that they were not a professionally religious group. They were a lay-led movement whose members lived ordinary lives, in which the reality of their faith could be played out on a daily basis in their interactions with others. So not only did Paul learn something about cultural engagement here, but the Pharisees also taught him the value of ministry being self-financing and rooted in everyday life.

In terms of his attitude to the culture and, therefore, to mission, Paul remained a Pharisee throughout his life. The one thing that changed everything was his encounter with the risen Christ on the road to Damascus. The passion that he displayed as a Christian apostle ran deep through his personality, and it is impossible to understand him apart from it. Passionate commitment is the one quality that characterised him from start to finish. His first appearance on the pages of the New Testament is as a witness to and collaborator in the death of Stephen (Acts 7:58—8:1), and, following the dispersal of Christians from Jerusalem, it was his passion for faith that motivated him to pursue them as far as Damascus (Acts 9:1–2; Galatians 1:13–14). To his great surprise, it was in the very act of being faithful that he found himself on the wrong side of God, and his world was turned upside down as he came to terms with new understandings of Jesus, of community, of tradition, of morality—indeed, of God. We would hope that none of today's pioneer ministers will find themselves so thoroughly wrongfooted, but there is a careful balance to be observed between being passionate about a cause and being self-opinionated in such a way that there is no room for further learning. Paul discounted the wisdom of Gamaliel (himself a prominent Pharisee: Acts 5:33–39) in the mistaken belief that, without his endeavours, God's work would never be accomplished.

This is the story of many enthusiasts. It is easy to imagine that the work of the Spirit depends on us, when sometimes we need to take a step backward and acknowledge that issues that seem black-and-white to us can often be far more complex—and that God might actually be doing some things of which the tradition disapproves. One of my friends is Barry Taylor, a musician, theologian and priest in the American Episcopal Church. He came to faith while working with AC/DC on their *Highway to Hell* tour in 1979. The very title of the tour was calculated to convince many Christians that, whatever was going on, it was nothing to do with God, and Barry tells how many of the venues were picketed by Christians warning of the spiritual dangers within. What was actually happening within was that he was reading his Bible in every spare minute he could find, and reflecting on the big questions of life that his experience in working with the band had identified.[11] Christians who were no doubt good and certainly passionate people thought they were doing God's work by protesting, when actually God was already at work in ways they could never have comprehended. It was something like that for Paul on the Damascus road, as he realised that God works in the most unexpected ways and often seems to break what we think are the rules in doing so.

Paul and his mission

Jesus advised his disciples always to be ready to read 'the signs of the times' (Matthew 16:1–3; 25:1–13), an instruction that is, no doubt, open to several different meanings—though one of them must surely be an exhortation to think strategically when it comes to mission. When we look at Paul from this angle, it becomes obvious that his mission activities were never random but always the outcome of careful strategic planning. He knew how to read the culture, including especially mundane aspects of everyday life. One of the great benefits of the Roman Empire was its transportation system, which offered easy access to the major centres of population, whether by road or by sea. Travel was not always straightforward and could be positively dangerous, but it was also facilitated by the common language of Greek that was spoken and understood everywhere. Paul recognised the communication channels of his day and used them appropriately. Communication today is very different from anything he could have imagined, but comparable opportunities of travel and conversation are all around us.

In addition, though, Paul read the culture more deeply. Tarsus was much like other major cities then and now, and gave him an awareness of the social unease that existed throughout the empire, as people struggled with issues of mobility, corruption, racial and class divisions, pluralism—all of which, in one form or another, are still with us today.[12] People were ready for a change, open to a different way of being. Tarsus was home to one or two significant Stoics, and their speculations (along with the theories of other philosophers of the day) had undermined much traditional belief so that belief in the old deities of Greece and Rome was no longer an option, though at the same time most ordinary people found the new philosophical nostrums impossible to comprehend. There was a spiritual vacuum in which it seemed that the old certainties were no longer believable but there was no widely embraced alternative. Into this vacuum came a plethora of mystical speculations based on traditional mythologies as well as imports from the east, which combined to form the popular spirituality of the so-called mystery religions.

If this scenario sounds familiar, then so it should. For many people today, 'science' has undermined our inherited faith traditions, but there is still a lively interest in 'spirituality' and there is no shortage of 21st-century 'mystery religions'. There is one obvious difference now, for, in the first century, Judaism and Christianity were both rooted in the eastern empire and engendered the same curiosity as the worship of Isis and other traditional Egyptian deities. They represented something esoteric and novel and, for that reason, held an attraction for the spiritual searchers of the day. Things are bound to be different in our post-Christian culture, although the growing interest in more mystical and contemplative forms of Christian faith may well be a manifestation of the same thing.[13] But Paul was also conscious of relating the gospel to some of the hard realities of life in his world, including the renewed search for values in a culture that had largely lost its moral compass, as well as affirming the spiritual importance of embodied life in the face of a pervasive Platonism that was world-denying and therefore struggled to speak to the everyday practical concerns of the average citizen. He also recognised the significance of population movements from the countryside into the cities, and the opportunities for the creation of new forms of community in such a setting. Urbanisation and population movements are still some of the biggest opportunities for mission in today's world.

Not only did Paul know how to read the culture, but he also went on to identify the possibilities that he could himself exploit. He was openly self-reflective about what he could not do, as well as what he could. As a Roman citizen he enjoyed privileges that were not open to other apostles, and he regarded this not as something to be ashamed of but as an opportunity to open doors to meet with the movers and shakers of his society. Moreover, he was clearly relatively well off, as he seems to have financed his extensive travels himself, accompanied by his personal entourage, including a physician in the shape of Luke. There can be a tendency among some pioneers today to understand Jesus' statements about the poor in a way that, in practice, leads to almost a refusal to connect with those who are perceived to be privileged. All of Jesus' disciples of whom we know anything beyond their names were key players in their social context, some of them running businesses with their own employees—most obviously Peter, James and John, who were able to give up work for weeks on end in order to spend time with Jesus, but whose businesses continued in their absence so that they were able to return to them whenever they chose to do so. Like Jesus before him, Paul recognised the importance of sharing the gospel with those who could make a difference on the civic stage. This perception influenced his choice of towns and cities to visit, as he deliberately chose to go himself to provincial capitals where he would meet the sort of Roman officials who could determine local policy. In the process, and under different circumstances, he could converse as an equal with Sergius Paul in Cyprus (Acts 13:4–12) or with Gallio in Corinth (Acts 18:12–17), while some of the friends named in his letters appear to have been government officials who had become Christians.

Paul also knew what he was less able to do, and his policy of visiting provincial capitals was predicated on the assumption that, once a Christian community had been established in such places, he would trust those new converts to take the initiatives that would spread the message more widely in their area. The establishment of the church at Colossae would be one obvious example of that strategy—a city that Paul never visited himself but whose church was part of his network, established by Epaphras, who met Paul in Ephesus.

In both these respects, there are lessons that today's pioneers do well to learn: the importance of reaching key decision makers, and also of recognising what we cannot do ourselves. The terminology of the mixed economy identifies the importance not only of diversity in church styles, but also of gifting and opportunity. As Paul put it, 'not many of you were wise by human standards, not many were powerful, not many were of noble birth' (with the clear implication that some were)—though all relied on God for spiritual wisdom (1 Corinthians 1:26–31).

Paul may have been relatively well off, but that did not mean he was pretentious and out of touch—far from it. He understood the many diverse people groups that lived in a typical Roman city, and he worked alongside them in their different social circumstances. As he put it in writing to Corinth, he became 'all things to all people' (1 Corinthians 9:19–23). He knew the difference between the synagogue and the marketplace, and between the upmarket Roman villas and the dismal tenements that accommodated many workers in the Roman cities. The gospel message to synagogue worshippers was not the same as it was in the streets of Lystra or in the learned halls of the philosophers of Athens. Unlike the original disciples of Jesus, Paul was a city person and understood urban life. Roman cities struggled with many of the same issues that we see in cities today, as migrants from the countryside and all over the empire uprooted themselves in search of a better life. Suburban sprawl was unknown, and ancient cities tended to maintain existing boundaries, which meant that growing populations led to overcrowding and high population density. The richest had their own villas—some of them quite extensive as they could also provide housing for their employees—but most people lived as tenants in multi-storied tenements, often with only one room per family. The big villas had elaborate water and sewage systems, but not the tenements, and in this environment life was hard, often short and disease-ridden. Constant migration meant a lot of strangers living in communities where people hardly knew one another and had no extended families for support. There was also a huge mix of ethnic groups: Antioch, in the first century, had 18 ethnic quarters.

Paul was not only able but also willing to transcend these social divisions. A typical day of mission activity could consist of discussions with upper-class philosophers at their lecture halls, alongside physical labour at his own space in a tenement (where the ground floors would often consist of workshops with living space above). This work has conventionally been identified as 'tent-making', although, in other ancient texts, the word used to describe this occupation in the New Testament (*skenopoios*) most often describes someone who made scenery and costumes for the theatre, an occupation which itself would have straddled diverse worlds in the urban environment.

Throughout his endeavours, Paul's relationships with people were central. Reading his letters, it is easy to form the impression that he offered a very wordy understanding of the gospel. The letters were written to people who were already Christians and, very often, in response to particular questions they had asked him, which inevitably determined the topics on which he wrote and the way in which he expressed himself. The truth is that we have only limited indications of how he went about the missional task, although there is one passage in his letters and one episode in Acts that might give us a good idea of his fundamental approach. He begins 1 Thessalonians by reflecting on the impact that these new Christians had made in their community in something like the six months since he had first met them, and the one thing he singles out is the relational attitude that he and his co-workers adopted in their ministry: 'We were gentle among you, like a nurse tenderly caring for her own children... determined to share with you not only the gospel of God but also our own selves... like a father with his children, urging and encouraging you' (1 Thessalonians 2:7–12).

We can be sure that this was an accurate description of his approach; otherwise the advice he offers later in the letter would have fallen on deaf ears. The language he uses is remarkable for several reasons, not only its gender inclusiveness (comparing his approach not just to any woman but to a breast-feeding mother) but, above all, the emphasis on relationships as central to effective evangelism. Paul knew what more recent Christians have often forgotten: that we have something to share with others not because we are different but because we are no different. Our struggles are the same as those of other people, with the same potential for disintegration and failure. The good news is not 'We have it, and you need it', but 'Life is hard and messy, but following Jesus makes a difference.' This realistic understanding of the human—

and Christian—condition comes across not only here but in many other passages in his letters, where Paul is open about his own weakness and vulnerability, yet confident that God is to be found through it all.

The other example of Paul's approach comes from the book of Acts, with Luke's account of his visit to Athens (Acts 17:16–34). This is not the place for an extensive reflection on his approach there, and, in any case, I have written about it elsewhere.[14] But as an example of sharing faith in a culture where traditional religious belief was passé and interest in the spiritual was high, his general attitude is worth noting. His encounter with the people of Athens begins with fear, which soon turns to a recognition that listening will be primary as he spends a number of days just hanging out in the city and observing its life. In accordance with the advice given by Jesus to the disciples (Luke 10:8–11), he waits to be invited to speak, and, when he does speak, he affirms the spiritual search of the culture by recognising the importance of the 'unknown god' and unhesitatingly adopting that language as an appropriate way to speak of Jesus. Although Luke gives only a summary of Paul's message, it is obvious that he must have told the story of Jesus, as he is subsequently quizzed about the resurrection. Significantly, in doing all this he not only affirms the popular spirituality represented by the unknown god, but also refers happily to pagan poets and philosophers, while not once referring to the Hebrew scriptures, even though we know from elsewhere how important they were to his wider understanding of the gospel.

Undergirding all of this must surely be a recognition of what we now call the *missio Dei*, the expectation that God would be at work in Athens—indeed, was already there in the guise of the 'unknown god'—and that the missional task was to recognise God's activity and presence, and to work alongside it. There is no missional pioneer today who does not need to learn all those lessons, and it is when we ignore or forget them that we imperil the mission itself.

Lessons from Paul

There are, then, many lessons to be learnt from Paul as a missional pioneer. There is a grand invitation and challenge to focus always and only on the basics of our message and our calling, and to do so with passion and energy, while recognising our own weakness and vulnerability. Then there is the question of culture and language. Increasingly, today's missional language in the global village is English: one of the surprising growth points in recent years has been English-speaking churches in Europe, who find that this is the shared language between east and west. But there is also the need for us to engage with the diverse cultural languages of the day—movies, music, social networking and so on.

We need to recognise that, when all is said and done, Christians are not a race apart but share in all the struggles and tragedies of humanity more generally. In the words of advice attributed to Dietrich Bonhoeffer, 'We should give up the foolish task of trying to be saints and get on with the more important task of being fully human.' The emotions displayed by Paul in the course of his ministry reflect that task very well, as he is at one moment lively and enthusiastic and at another defeated and depressed—and sometimes experiencing all those emotions and more at the same time. Which of us has not been there? But underlying it all is his confidence that the work to which he was committed is, in the end, not dependent on him but is a genuine work of the Spirit of Christ, who constantly takes him into dangerous and scary places while at the same time empowering him in unimaginable ways (Philippians 4:13). Mention of the Spirit, finally, reminds me that any effective ministry will always be grounded in personal spirituality and faithfulness to Christ—and that might be the most important lesson of all.

Notes

1   *Mission-Shaped Church*, p. v.

2   Steven Croft, *Jesus' People: What the church should do next* (CHP, 2009).

3   Most stridently by Michael Frost & Alan Hirsch, *The Shaping of Things to Come* (Hendrickson, 2003), pp. 111–133; Alan Hirsch, *The Forgotten Ways: Reactivating the missional church* (Brazos, 2007), pp. 142–144.

4   Marcus J Borg & John Dominic Crossan, *The First Paul* (SPCK, 2009), p. 11.

5   For an accessible account, see N.T. Wright, *Paul in Fresh Perspective* (Fortress Press, 2009).

6   For a missional perspective, however, see Eckhard J. Schnabel, *Paul the Missionary* (IVP, 2008).

7   Walter Wink, *The Bible in Human Transformation* (Fortress Press, 2nd edn 2010), pp. 1–2.

8   Borg & Crossan, *The First Paul*, p. 11.

9   Colossians and Romans are exceptions, although Paul wrote Romans to correct some mistaken impressions about him, spread there by his opponents, and to prepare the ground for a personal visit. The church at Colossae had been founded by one of his converts in Ephesus, so there was a close personal connection already.

10 It also featured as the theme music for the popular TV series 'Joan of Arcadia' (2003–2005) and in Tom Shadyac's 2003 film *Bruce Almighty*.

11 Barry Taylor, *Singing in the Dark* (Kingsway, 1990).

12 See Gregory S. Aldrete, *Daily Life in the Roman City* (University of Oklahoma Press, 2004); Helmut Koester, *Paul and His World* (Fortress Press, 2007); S.E. Porter (ed.), *Paul's World* (Brill, 2008); John Drane, *The World of the Bible* (Lion Hudson, 2009), pp. 184–247; Simon Jones, *The World of the Early Church* (Lion Hudson, 2011).

13 See Steven Croft & Ian Mobsby (eds.), *Fresh Expressions in the Sacramental Tradition* (Canterbury Press, 2009).

14 John Drane, *Do Christians Know How to Be Spiritual?* (DLT, 2005), pp. 111–120.

A pioneer's story

I'm part of the Norwich Christian Meditation Centre, where we engage with 'spiritual searchers', recognising that most are looking anywhere and everywhere for answers to their spiritual questions—everywhere except the church, that is. So we use ancient meditative traditions and monastic practices to show them that Christianity does have something to say to their searching. We run courses, host speakers and hold two different Christian meditation groups, as well as having a small Sunday morning congregation. We envisage all the expressions of the meditation centre as tiles in a mosaic, creating a whole community greater than the sum of its parts.

I developed an alternative worship community called Ambient Wonder, alongside someone else who shared my vision of connecting people who attended other groups with the Christian story in more relevant ways. We had a strong desire to engage the whole person in worship and break down the dualism that exists between what happens in church and what's going on in the rest of our lives. We wanted to create space for people to connect with God, rather than prescribe a route for that journey to take. We wanted to use every bit of ourselves by being creative and seeing where it took us.

The response from churched people has been mixed: many describe it as 'DIY worship', which they find hard after a lifetime of being directed and passively receiving what someone else has prepared. Others love the freedom it brings. But it's not intended for churched people, so we have constantly tried to push outwards, honouring the Sunday congregation that supported us when we first began but moving away into spaces that are less driven by the unconscious assumptions about worship held by many Christians.

In fact, this has been one of the biggest challenges of the past five years: we've had to be constantly alert to the pull to make Ambient Wonder safer or more comfortable for those in church already, and determinedly making it more connected with everyday culture and those who don't know God's story.

The other main challenge has been developing as a community rather than just a bunch of people who plan and run events. We are completely open to anyone who wants to join in with planning and creating parts of the events. If they are interested in the theme, they can join us to eat pizza and drink wine and brainstorm ideas for the next event. People drift in and out from month to month, depending on their other commitments or whether they're interested in the theme. On one level we enjoy the freedom that approach offers, but at the same time it does make it hard to establish real relationships.

We've never had a hierarchical leadership: I and a couple of others facilitate the group by getting dates on the calendar, keeping the website and Facebook page up to date, and publicising events. But the themes are chosen by those who show up to the social gathering where we plan the term ahead, and then curators are responsible for pulling together the ideas and contributions of others to ensure that each event makes sense and is accessible to people, regardless of whether they've been before. We've always taken the issue of power seriously, seeking to give it away with open hands and let people grow by taking responsibility.

Because of the transitory nature of the group who would consider themselves Ambient Wonder, there will be issues of sustainability, should any of the three facilitators move on. So we're entering a phase in which we have to be more deliberate about the leadership functions that need to be carried, and see how the group responds. We're also going to experiment with being less events-focused, to see what it would look like if we applied the principles we've developed to guide our worship to the way we live our lives more generally.

So a new phase in the journey awaits. We're not sure if Ambient Wonder will be a permanent fixture in the landscape of the Meditation Centre, or whether it will turn out to have been a learning experience that has broadened our understanding of worship and enabled us to grow in our understanding of how God connects with people outside the familiar structures of church. Either way, it provides a space for exploration of God's story for those who've never encountered it before, and a place of connectedness between our worship and the whole of our lives.

Heather Cracknell is one of the leaders of Ambient Wonder, an alternative worship community in Norwich. For more information, visit www. ambientwonder.org and www.norwichmeditation.co.uk.

11

Wild or tamed: the dangers of domesticating pioneers

Mark Russell

Sitting in a coffee shop in Sheffield, I was talking about the state of play at the end of the first phase of the Fresh Expressions project, along with my colleague the Revd Canon Dr George Lings, who leads Church Army's Research Unit, The Sheffield Centre. His analysis was that it felt as if we were at half-time in a game of football, and ahead on goals. I agree with him: we have seen much progress in the past few years.

Since the publication of the *Mission-Shaped Church* report[1] there has been a much greater understanding of what Archbishop Rowan Williams calls 'the mixed economy church'. It is always good to take a moment to see just how far we have come. I rejoice that fresh expressions of church have popped up across the country, different Christian denominations have partnered for the journey, the Church of England has introduced a stream of ordination ministry for pioneers, the Mission-Shaped Ministry course has introduced many people to pioneering concepts, the advent of the Bishops' Mission Order has resulted in pioneering Christian communities being legally recognised as churches in their own right, and mission agencies like Church Army (which I lead), have reorientated their priorities for pioneering mission. As I reflect on all that has been achieved, I rejoice and thank God.

Sometimes people think fresh expressions are merely a fad that will pass. They think that, somehow, all this work is a panic measure taken by a church faced with falling numbers. The Archbishop of Canterbury addressed this belief head-on at the launch of the Mission-Shaped Questions book in 2008, when he said, speaking of the Fresh Expressions movement:

Fresh Expressions is not a desperate panic strategy to shore up a crumbling institution. Fresh Expressions is about the rediscovery of the deepest roots of who we are as Christians, as people who belong to a living church which is the body of a living Christ. That's what Fresh Expressions is for. And that means, of course, it's not simply for a group of Café Church attenders here or surfers there or whatever; it's for all of us. The now extremely shop-soiled phrase 'mixed economy' does remind us that what this is about is recalling the Church to what I think I might call an excellence of service, praying that God will give us that quality of excellence of edge and depth in all that we do, whether it is received ways of being church or new and exploratory ways of being church— what we want is edge and depth, and that surely has to be good news for the whole of the Church of England.[2]

In the same set of remarks, the Archbishop wanted to ensure that we help people emerging from fresh expressions to go on and plant their own pioneering Christian communities. He asked, 'How do you move people on from being the recipients to being those who themselves grow into a real Christian fullness such that they themselves can take on the transforming work?'[3]

The identification of people with the gifts and heart for pioneering was central to the recommendations of the Mission-Shaped Church working party. George Lings has developed this thinking in his own chapter in this book, but it is useful to remember what the report actually said.

The text reads:

The Ministry Division of the Archbishops' Council should actively seek to encourage the identification, selection and training of pioneer church planters, for both lay and ordained ministries, through its appropriate channels to bishops' selectors, diocesan Reader Boards and training institutions. Specific selection criteria should be established. Patterns of training should reflect the skills, gifting and experiences of those being trained.[4]

However, George Lings' comments to me over coffee implicitly reveal that there are some areas where we have not made as much progress as we could have done. One key point I wish to advance is that the church risks domesticating its pioneers. To consider this point, I want to try to set in context some of the questions we need to ask, to make progress in the 'second half' of the Fresh Expressions game.

In the Church of England there are now a number of pathways for pioneers. One is to seek ordination as an Ordained Pioneer Minister (OPM), another is as a lay pioneer, and another as a Church Army Evangelist. There are three common issues facing all pioneer pathways, namely selection, training and deployment. If we want to avoid the domestication of pioneers, we have to make further progress with all three.

Selection

There is a concern that there are very few pioneers involved as selectors for Ordained Pioneer Ministry. Bishops' selectors are wise and able people, but can they identify a pioneer? In Church Army, we always have a pioneering evangelist on our selection panels, as it sometimes takes one pioneer to spot another. Frequently, by nature, they are edgy and riskier candidates; they are a little more 'rough round the edges'. There is a concern in some quarters that genuine pioneers might not pass the selection criteria!

At the same time, pioneers are not just 'wacky' people. They need an understanding of contemporary cultures, an ability to listen and discern God's voice in different contexts, and an ability to grow a relevant expression of Christian community that reaches people with the good news. Pioneers understand that 'off the shelf' solutions do not work, but that a Christian community needs to emerge from excellent incarnational ministry. Pioneers must be good reflective practitioners, competent in holistic mission and able to spot opportunities. If you like, they need entrepreneurial flair. Many of us fear that what some selectors are looking for is good mission-minded clergy. That is, of course, a wonderful thing to look for, but good mission-minded clergy will find themselves drawn to inherited church rather than to pioneering contexts.

Training

If we want to train pioneers properly, some of us contend that this cannot be adequately done in a lecture room. Many leading thinkers in these matters believe, as do I, that pioneers need to train in an action/reflection or apprenticeship model of learning, working alongside an experienced practitioner. Church Army responded to this belief by making the transition from a residential college to 'Mission-based training' in 2008. It was a huge and costly decision, but one that we believe to have been right. Our frontline evange-lists were telling us that we needed to train people in a holistic way, integrating study, action and reflection. Church Army trainees now work towards a Foundation Degree in Evangelism, weaving theology and praxis together, and working in a Centre of Mission alongside experienced evangelists.[5] When we were developing our syllabus, we worked with a number of our pioneers to write a Competency Framework, which outlined the skills set and tool kit we wanted every pioneering evangelist to have, and then worked backwards to design the curriculum that would train a pioneer in those competencies.

Many pioneers are training in a 'chalk and talk' model, not hugely different from 'regular' ordination training, with a few bolt-on modules in pioneering. The view seems to be that OPMs need to be able to minister as priests in parishes as well as in pioneering contexts. This is intended to make the priest more deployable. One pioneer ordinand told me, 'I am not sure if my training is neutering me or neutralising me.' Another trainee pioneer said that she felt she was being taught by people who had no real conceptual understanding of pioneering. Another commented that her tutor had told her the aim of the training was to make her into a priest who could work anywhere. If we are concerned about the domestication of pioneers, we need to consider carefully how they are trained.

I would argue that if we are really selecting pioneers for training, they should not easily fit into an inherited context, but should be released and given permission to work outside the inherited model, pioneering new ways to be church.

Deployment

The third element of pioneer ministry is perhaps the key area where the risk of domestication of pioneers is strongest. The wider church has been facing significant resource challenges. Within Church Army over the past few years, we have had to reorientate our entire organisation to face mission in this new paradigm. We have had to make tough decisions and choose how to spend our money in such a way as to promote more pioneering frontline mission. As a leader, my budget is the single biggest lever I can use to effect change. I recently challenged a bishop to consider whether or not his budget reflected his priorities. He concluded that it didn't, and he is now in the process of reorientating his budget to spend more funds on fresh expressions of church.

There is a perception that when push comes to shove, the

church will safeguard the inherited church model and sacrifice the pioneering. It's not that the church doesn't value pioneering work, just that with limited resources the parish system will be maintained first. All these pressures work together to risk drawing the pioneer out of church planting contexts into the inherited model.

Many pioneers find themselves in lonely contexts, with little pastoral support. They find themselves as members of local clergy meetings in Deanery Chapters, with other clergy who are exhausted from maintaining the edifice of the parish system. I realise that this chapter is about the risk of domesticating pioneers, but let me pause here and make the point that the leaders of inherited church also feel weary and undervalued. I have had the privilege of addressing a number of clergy conferences across the world over the past three years, and have met so many parish clergy who are just exhausted from the pressures of parish life. Many of those clergy are leading multi-parish benefices. They are not only burning their candle at both ends; they have cut their candle in half and are burning it at all four ends. Yet these very busy clergy simply don't understand the mission that the pioneer is undertaking. This results in the pioneers feeling lonely, guilty, misunderstood and under huge pressure to deliver. They feel that unless they can point to a church plant, their future is in doubt. Many of them have been sent to posts on 3- to 5-year contracts, which fail to recognise that pioneering is long-term work. Quite frankly, it is hard work.

We are familiar with the parable of the sower (Matthew 13: 1–23), in which the sower sows seed on different kinds of soil. Often, a pioneer seeking to grow a fresh expression in an un-churched area finds not soil but concrete. It can take years just to break down the concrete, to reveal the soil, before the tending and sowing can even begin. In Church Army we are now budgeting for pioneering posts to be held over 5–7 years. I love the Lighthouse Project in Southampton, led by my friend Tim Hyde, a very gifted Church Army Evangelist. Tim has an allotment project, which has involved taking some rough ground, caring for it, tending it and growing new plants to bless the local community. It feels like a modern-day outworking of Jesus' parable.

Many pioneers are anxious that, with financial pressures facing the church, there will be pressure on stipendary pioneering posts in the future. I have had a number of pioneers tell me that their bishop has tried to suggest they move to a half-time post in a parish. These are signs of pioneers being drawn into the inherited church, which I would argue is a form of domestication.

To avoid this, we need a fresh understanding of pioneering in the wider church. We need leaders who recognise that pioneering ministry is long-term work, that it needs a skills set frequently different from that required by pastoral ministry, and that pioneers need supportive, permission-giving leaders. So, to minimise the risk of the domestication of pioneers, I suggest we need to make progress in a number of areas.

1. We need to work on our theology

In his fascinating book *Church Planting: Laying Foundations*,[6] Stuart Murray writes that church plants operate in a theological framework that is often assumed rather than articulated. He argues that we need to think out our theology of church planting very carefully, otherwise it will hinder the long-term impact of our work.

My concern is that some fresh expressions of church have been created to provide a place for Christians who cannot find another church to belong to. That is, in itself, no bad thing. But there is a risk that people will think Café Church or Messy Church is a good thing, so they set up a similar initiative in their area, without really addressing the needs of unchurched people locally. The Mission-Shaped Church report argues that fresh expressions need to have an incarnational agenda—going into a community and living among people, to serve, bless and listen. It is from those relationships that pioneers can seek to grow a church community that ministers to those people. The term 'double listening' is often used to describe the pioneer's process of listening to Christian tradition and to God, but also listening to the cultural context.

Church planting is not an end in itself; it is only one part of the mission of God, the *missio dei*. Our church planting is God's mission, working to God's agenda. God is the missionary, as Murray puts it:

God's missionary purposes are cosmic in scope, concerned with the restoration of all things, the establishment of shalom, the renewal of creation, and the coming of the Kingdom of God, as well as the redemption of fallen humanity and the building of the church. Mission is defined, directed, energised and accomplished by God.[7]

Put bluntly, I believe that the very term 'fresh expressions' could now be seen as unhelpful. When bishops in England tell me they are very excited that 30 per cent of their parishes are engaged with fresh expressions, I want to panic. What I think they mean is that 30 per cent of the clergy ticked the 'Fresh expression' box on the archdeacon's visitation form. It means, perhaps, that a thoughtful, well-intentioned priest has brought a drum kit into the 11am service, or provided coffee and a doughnut afterwards, or, like one parish I heard of, put up a new noticeboard outside. I am worried that the language has been cheapened. The idea of an emerging Christian community being grown in a new place, after missional work, is being blurred by the modernisation of inherited churches' acts of worship. Of course, the modernisation of the church's acts of worship is a good idea, but it is not a pioneering fresh expression of church.

This leads me to another concern: do church leaders always 'get' the concept of fresh expressions? One pioneer gave me a great illustration to make this point. She said that she has a basic understanding of the French language. When overseas, she can order food and make basic conversation, but the jokes go over her head. She wonders if some church leaders have a rudimentary understanding of pioneering but don't really understand what makes a pioneer tick.

Church planting and fresh expressions need to be rooted in incarnational theology and in the theology of missio dei, otherwise our pioneering risks being seen simply as a way for the church to shore up its membership and pay its bills.

Murray puts it this way:

The broad scope of missio dei *must not be reduced to evangelism or church planting. Church planting is legitimate only if set within a broader mission context. Divorced from this context, church planting may represent little more than ecclesiastical expansionism.*[8]

2. We need to get location right

Where do we pioneer new work? Is it where pioneers themselves feel comfortable? I worry that many fresh expressions are in middle-class areas, and for white people. I admit that I am middle-class and my church is mostly white. However, we need to locate pioneers who can plant fresh expressions with people of different ethnic groups and in areas of social deprivation. I met an amazing guy living in Belfast, who has planted a fresh expression of church with African people in Belfast! My friend Alan Park is a Church Army Evangelist who runs a fresh expression on a bus in Chesterfield, which is a church community for homeless people.

Interestingly, the Spirit told the church at Antioch to set apart Barnabas and Saul for the work God had called them to, but with no clear instructions about where to go. They chose Cyprus, as Acts 4:36 tells us that Barnabas came from that island. Alan Park, who runs the homeless fresh expression, was once himself a homeless man. Yet we have also seen white middle-class pioneers living and working alongside marginalised non-white people.

That leads me to another question. How do we do fresh expressions in deprived areas? Across the UK there are tough areas, social housing areas, where in many cases the church has backed off. I believe that only the fresh expressions agenda will engage those areas with the gospel. To avoid the domestication of pioneers, we need to think afresh about where we pioneer.

3. We need to sustain the pioneer's spirit

My mentor once told me that you cannot give what you haven't got. Pioneering is hard work—often lonely and thankless work. Frequently, results take a lot of time to be seen, and we can get discouraged. The fledgling communities we grow are often fragile. How can we help pioneers to sustain their work? Where do pioneers worship? How can we grow mission accompaniers to walk with pioneers? How can we help pioneers not to burn out? Leaders need to sustain their pioneers, and dumping them in the local clergy chapter meeting will not do. To avoid the domestication of pioneers, we need to nourish them, feed their souls, and enable them to carry out their ministry for the long haul.

Jesus sent his disciples out two by two, yet we often send our pioneers out one by one. To sustain pioneers and to avoid domestication, we need to get away from the model of the lone pioneer.

Rahm Emmanuel, formerly Chief of Staff to President Obama, says, 'Never waste a crisis.' The church in the UK faces a form of crisis. I do not believe we can sustain the top-heavy machine of dioceses and parishes. We are placing all our clergy under incredible strains; there are fewer and fewer of them and they are running more and more parishes. Something has to give. We need leaders in our dioceses who will make changes, take risks and free up people and money to do mission work, not just maintain the monolith of the church machine.

Two years ago, I brought Jackie Pullinger to speak to the Church Army staff conference at Swanwick. I wanted to ask her to challenge us about mission, evangelism, taking risks and God's heart for the poor. After I had introduced her, as my assembled colleagues applauded, her first words were, 'I'm sorry to be here.' She said she'd been sure that Jesus would have returned by now. That sentence changed my life. What would look different in our ministry and our church structure if we genuinely believed that Jesus was coming back tomorrow? The vision of a mixed economy church calls us to value our traditional churches and work hard to renew and revive our inherited church. Yet it also calls us to resource and encourage the development of fresh expressions as new and emerging Christian communities which can reach places and people that inherited church cannot. We need to resource, nourish and nurture leaders of inherited church, and we need to free up and release pioneers. We need to select and train people specifically for each different task. I dare to believe that we can do both.

Notes

1 G. Cray (ed.), *Mission-Shaped Church* (CHP, 2004).
2 See www.archbishopofcanterbury.org/1595.
3 www.archbishopofcanterbury.org/1595.
4 Cray, *Mission-Shaped Church*, p. 147.
5 See www.churcharmy.org.uk/mbt.
6 Stuart Murray, *Church Planting: Laying Foundations* (Herald Press, 2001).
7 Murray, *Church Planting*, p. 31
8 Murray, *Church Planting*, p. 32

12

Making us tick: the psychology of pioneers

Kate Middleton

Church leadership is a profession with a long and detailed history. As long as records have been kept, there has been a rich tradition of individuals who, with or without training, have devoted their lives to working inside the church. Following in the footsteps of the disciples who gave up their previous professions to become leaders in the early church, many people find themselves in a position where volunteering and running ministries in their spare time develops until they become full-time church leaders or ministers. Still more make a decision early in life to make this their career, and undergo formal training to become ordained ministers of one kind or another.

However, working in church leadership is never easy. As a profession, it demands perhaps a wider range of skills and abilities than any other, and combines them with long and often unsociable hours. Statistically, church leaders are one of the professional groups most at risk of struggling with psychological and emotional problems related to their job. Research suggests that nearly three-quarters of full-time church leaders admit to experiencing stress levels so high that they consider moving to another profession. Almost all have known colleagues who have suffered serious physical or emotional illness related to stress. Many feel that their ministry has had serious damaging effects on their life at home—for example, their relationship with their families and their marriages—and there are examples of well-known leaders who have seen private tragedy in their lives exist alongside their successful leadership careers.

As we strive to understand the challenges of the environment in which leaders work, we also need to consider the mechanisms that underlie problems when they develop. More than that, we need to be able to identify potential issues and worrying patterns of behaviour early, so that intervention can be implemented and given the best chance of success. There may also be an argument for influencing formal procedures such as selection or training. Of course, the vast majority of people in full-time leadership find themselves following in the footsteps of many others whose wisdom and collective experiences already inform training and selection, as well as producing good resources and support systems and ultimately guiding new leaders along in their journey. But this challenge is particularly key for pioneer leaders, who are the trail-blazers in a new form of ministry. There is no doubt that pioneering a new ministry is an exhausting and demanding experience, but does this mean that those who go into pioneer ministry are at any greater risk than any other church leaders? Are the issues they face the same as those encountered by their colleagues'? Do they experience the issues in greater depth, or are there different problems altogether?

As the picture of church leadership begins to change dramatically, is there a risk that the demands—and therefore the negative consequences—might become more widespread? Are we at risk of producing a model of leadership that is unsustainable, with a generation of short-term leaders who set up and pioneer great things but are then unable to continue in the work because of the toll it takes on them?

Although the pioneering journey is different for each individual and ministry, there are common themes and stages. Therefore, as we think about the specific demands that may be placed on pioneers, it is valuable to consider each stage in turn. What can our knowledge about people in general teach us about expectations for our pioneers? Can we gain clues from other professions, which will help us to predict when and where problems may lie?

Stage 1: The call: why you and not someone else?

In some ways, the first and most important stage for a pioneering minister takes place long before they actually do anything. This stage is all about why they do whatever it is they end up doing. Church leadership in general stands apart from many other career paths because it stems from more than just a 'head'-based decision. Few people treat it as 'just' a job. The vast majority talk of it in terms of a calling. Like Paul, who introduces himself in his letters in terms of his role and ministry, their role is more than just their job: it is part of who they are and their reason for being. This tends to be the case particularly for people who are working in pioneer ministry. They are doing what they do because they feel sure it is 'what they were meant to do'.

Psychologically, certain issues spring from this position. The first is that experiencing a job, task or ministry as a 'calling' means that there is a lot of passion associated with it. This may be a positive emotion, driving people towards their aims, but it also can stem from a negative emotional reaction—an empathy with the suffering that people endure or the difficult situations in which they find themselves. Nehemiah describes how he was overcome with weeping (Nehemiah 1:4) and found himself in a state of mourning for the situation he saw in Jerusalem. This was what motivated him to seek God and eventually take on a leadership role among the people of the ruined city. He saw tragedy around him and he wanted to do something about it.

Pioneering ministries spring from the heart and often involve this kind of visceral (emotional) draw. This sort of motive to ministry is very powerful and, of course, often God-given. Indeed, many renowned speakers have called on leaders to seek out these emotional responses to the world they seek to change and see them as a key part of developing a ministry.[1] Such powerful reactions will enable an individual to persist in pursuing a goal in the face of obstacles or challenges—something that may well be a vital skill in pioneering new forms of church.

At the same time, there are potential problems associated with decisions or goals that carry such a great emotional load. The psychological impact is clear in the kind of language people use: many will talk of feeling that they are 'carrying a burden' for a particular situation or group of people, and the empathetic responses they describe, like Nehemiah's, often use powerful words like 'anguish', 'sorrow' and 'aching'. The view may develop that the stronger this response, the better, in terms of the strength of someone's calling or determination to have an impact in the work they plan to do. We must be sure, however, that these powerful reactions are indeed God-given and not triggered by something else entirely. In fact, there is evidence that, for some people, very strong emotional or empathetic responses can be a sign of personality factors that leave them especially at risk of emotional problems such as anxiety and depression.[2] Furthermore, experiencing such a strong emotional drive can push people to work beyond sensible limits, as well as meaning that their stress response is magnified— all of which leaves them more prone to burn-out. God-given drives are powerful, but even Jesus took time out in the face of overwhelming need (see Luke 5:15–17). Certainly, wisdom from other caring professions would caution us that people who carry these great emotional burdens may be more at risk of 'compassion fatigue', which may limit the length of time they can continue to work in an emotionally demanding field.[3]

The second risk for people who find their 'job' becoming such a large part of who they are involves the subtle but powerful ways in which we view ourselves and ultimately construct our self-esteem or self-identity. The foundations of self-esteem are created in childhood but they are built upon and developed during adolescence and into adulthood. Most healthy adults find that their self-esteem is made up of around six different parts, which consist of input and feedback from various different sources. Some come from your own opinions or perceptions—your concept of whether you are a 'good person' or not, your academic ability (in other words, how clever you think you are), what you think of your physical appearance and so on. Others come from the people around us—the opinions of those closest to us, which matter the most to us. Finally, there are real-life indicators, such as performance in work or other environments (competitions and so on). Most people find that some element, at least, of their self-esteem is based on how they compare themselves with others.

For most people, their self-esteem is fairly well balanced, meaning that no one segment carries much more weight than any other. Problems tend to occur if, for whatever reason, an individual's self-esteem becomes too dependent on any one factor. A child growing up in a very competitive family, for example, may become an adult who bases a lot of their self-esteem on winning—with inevitable problems should they ever be at risk of not coming first. Someone else might find that their self-esteem is based far too strongly on their physical appearance, leading them to become very anxious if they feel they do not look their best. A real risk in our very work- and career-focused culture is that people base too much of their self esteem on what they do. Our career or profession inevitably forms a part of who we are, but what if this part becomes too significant?

The risk, if our self-esteem is over-dependent on one area of life, is that when challenges or problems hit that area, we can feel that the fabric of our universe is collapsing. So, for some pioneers, their 'job' becomes part of who they are, and this makes them very vulnerable to becoming over-dependent on it. This can result in increased stress and anxiety, as well as a tendency for situations to trigger much greater emotional reactions than they otherwise would. It is very important that pioneers are encouraged to develop other aspects of their life, aside from their ministry. In this case, a good work–life balance is essential.

Stage 2: The environment: why here and not somewhere else?

A second question that is vital to ask of anyone considering pioneer ministry is 'What is calling them out of the traditional church?' It is important to know what motivates people to develop their own way of working rather than continuing 'within the system'. This question brings us to the huge array of research looking at entrepreneurial businesspeople—those who tend to develop their own ways of doing things and spot and exploit opportunities or gaps in the established system.

Often, at the root of such a move is 'disillusionment with the status quo'.[4] Pioneers tend to be very dynamic and well driven. They are wired to seek results, and to find new and innovative ways of getting those results if necessary. They can think outside the box and apply alternative perspectives and new ways of thinking to old problems. As such, pioneers need character qualities like creativity, as well as the confidence to put their ideas into practice. They may become frustrated with tradition ('We've been doing it this way for 100 years so we're not about to change now'), resistance to change ('Why should we look at new ways of doing things? We're quite happy with the way things are now') and compromise ('This will do—it's not ideal but it's good enough'). Pioneers can therefore be true visionaries, with a really positive outlook. However, it is vital that they are also able to follow things through and take the time to let things evolve. Business research describes so called 'enthusiastic entrepreneurs', who are great at creating new ideas but not so good at thinking about long-term success.[5] What pioneer ministries need is not just a great new idea but the ability to put time, effort and patience into letting the idea take form and develop.

Another potential issue surrounds the question of independence. Pioneers tend to enjoy working independently, setting their own deadlines and work structures. They are good at self-motivation and may prefer it to working under close supervision. These are good skills, but ultimately pioneer leaders do not work in a vacuum. In fact, they must juggle their independence and their need to be self-motivating and run their own work with the reality that, following the biblical model set by the early church in Acts, most need to continue working under some kind of formal church supervision. Most will talk readily about the added challenges this brings, and some may find the unexpected limitations very frustrating. In addition, there is a big difference between someone who *likes* to work independently and someone who *needs* to work independently. The latter will struggle to work within established hierarchies and may find it very difficult to accept guidance or supervision. For this reason, it is wise to be very cautious if problems to do with working as part of a team, or with the hierarchical nature of the traditional church, seem to form the basis of a desire to move outside it.

It is interesting also to consider the roots of a preference for working independently. Several entrepreneurs describe how their childhood experiences encouraged them to develop independence and work alone.[6] However, such experiences may have resulted in the development of other difficult issues or emotional Achilles' heels, which may become more serious issues when the person is placed into the pressure cooker that full-time pioneer ministry can be. One emotion, in particular, that can arise quickly when pressures and stresses become significant is frustration. Frustration is a great motivator for change, and many pioneers will admit that part of their early motivation was a frustration with the limitations of a more formal church setting. But frustration is likely to be a regular experience in setting up a pioneering ministry as well, so it is vital to think about how someone handles frustration when it hits. The ability to tolerate frustration and to learn ways of coping with it, rather than taking the opportunity to escape it, is probably key for most pioneers.[7]

Stage 3: The team: who are all these people?

The vast majority of successful new ventures in business are developed by teams rather than individuals acting alone,[8] and pioneer ministries are no exception. The most important factor in any pioneering ministry is therefore likely to be something more than just the individual who initiates it. It is essential that a pioneering leader can construct and then head up a successful team.

Perhaps the first challenge is in the early formation of a team. Most teams form around a leader who represents the same ideas as those held by the other people in the team: in other words, they are prototypical of the team ideal.[9] The risk in pioneer contexts is that the team begins to resemble one misfit leading a bunch of other misfits—at least from the perspective of the 'mother' church. This may feel threatening to those outside the pioneering team and can sometimes be interpreted as a criticism of more traditional formats. An alternative leadership pattern requires a pioneer to work and become established and respected within the traditional church first, before they can start to propose new ideas. Ultimately, the supervision and support (financial, if nothing else) of a parent church is likely to be crucial, so there are obvious advantages to this route. However, becoming respected from within the formal church takes time and will require the pioneer to manage many tricky emotions (especially frustration) during that 'foundation' period. Indeed, both leadership routes are likely to involve conflict situations, and a wise pioneer will have developed good skills to handle those conflicts well, ensuring that the solutions value both the people involved and the task at hand.

Whatever route is chosen, once a team is formed, many of the usual challenges of leadership will present themselves. Pioneer leaders cannot simply interest people in joining a leadership team, but need to manage their group effectively over the long term. This is important, as some character features that may initially appear very positive in a pioneer who is leading a group may be detrimental in the long term because they focus too much on that individual and too little on the team. These kinds of features might include those that could be seen as attention-seeking behaviour, as well as skills related to creating drama, or even what you might describe as flirtatious behaviour—which can be very effective in persuading people to join a team.[10] Good communication is crucial, particularly in a group leader who is aiming to spread their vision within the group.[11]

Another group of personality traits become very relevant in discussions about team dynamics and team leadership. There are many different personality traits that can affect people's ability to work well within a team, and some of them are related to the kind of skills that bring an individual into pioneer leadership in the first place. Perhaps the most well-known potential personality difference is the introversion–extraversion spectrum. Most experts agree that this trait has its roots in genuine differences in the baseline arousal of the brain. Some people have a lower baseline, and therefore enjoy particularly stimulating situations or circumstances that raise this baseline. We would describe these people as being more extravert, and they typically enjoy more vibrant surroundings, groups of people and louder or busier styles of worship or service in church. Meanwhile, introverts have a much higher baseline arousal, meaning that they are stimulated enough already and prefer quieter, more contemplative surroundings and service plans.

The frequency of introverts and extraverts among church

leaders is hotly debated by researchers in this area. Studies of leadership style, particularly transformational leadership, find that extraversion is correlated with measures of successful leadership, and that extraverts are more likely than introverts to emerge as leaders within a group.[12] Studies among church leaders tend to find mixed results, with some claiming a greater frequency of extraverted leaders and others identifying many introverted leaders. Several studies (including our own somewhat anecdotal research among pioneer leaders) find a good balance of introversion and extraversion (indeed, it is much more common to score somewhere in the middle than to be strongly introvert or extravert).

Whatever the frequency, introverted leaders are likely to need to take action to avoid problems associated with their psychological preference. Introverts are often deep thinkers, spending much more time analysing situations and needs, and may therefore be creative thinkers who are drawn to pioneering new ways of doing church. However, some will struggle to work within a team and communicate their vision effectively to others, and may also find conflict very difficult, preferring to avoid it altogether or simply cave in and accommodate the views of others. Those who do find strategies to enable them to communicate well may find that they consistently need to operate within very stimulating environments, which are not their natural domain. This means that they have to become very good at handling the higher levels of stress that their job triggers in them.

Another key personality trait is perfectionism. Perfectionism is a fascinating personality trait, which describes the degree to which someone demands increasingly high standards in everything they (and other people) do, in order to be satisfied.[13] Perfectionists push themselves very hard, and often set themselves increasingly challenging goals. They struggle to allow themselves to accept anything less than perfection and may work to the point of exhaustion in pursuit of it. Perfectionism is linked to great success, with many key figures from the world of business, sport and other domains scoring very high on measures of this trait. However, it has also been linked with great distress, seeming to trigger a greater risk of problems with stress, as well as emotional and psychological difficulties including anxiety, eating disorders and even suicidal thoughts.

Perfectionism is a key issue for pioneering ministers because it tends to be more common in any field where people are very driven and well-motivated. Perfectionists will not accept second-best and are wildly infuriated by the 'it will do' attitude. This is often linked in ministry with the frustration that can lead people to work outside the traditional church. Perfectionism creates key issues within a team and for the perfectionist individual. On the whole, working as or with a perfectionist increases stress levels, and this can become problematic. If unrealistic goals are set, they can lead to poor morale and even apathy, as they can make it feel as if a ministry is constantly failing, even when, in reality, it is achieving quite well. Some perfectionists struggle with team work as they find that other people rarely achieve the same standards as they themselves would have aimed for.

Overall, what is required in group formation and successful group leadership is a leader who has good awareness and understanding of the many psychological issues that can be part of working with a team. Charismatic leaders are generally agreed to require some or all of four key skills: learning to be accurate in the way they perceive others; learning how to communicate so that people perceive them in a positive way; learning to manage well in lots of different social situations; and learning to express themselves and their emotions well, so that they can induce enthusiasm in others.[14] Skills like these (and there is some evidence that they tend to be more naturally correlated with extraversion)[15] may well be essential for those wishing to be successful in developing pioneering leadership teams.

Stage 4: Lasting the course

Whatever the factors you consider important in the psychology of pioneering leaders, the reason it matters is that we need to be bringing forward leaders who are able to stay in ministry throughout their lives. As Paul states in his farewell to the Ephesian elders, 'I consider my life worth nothing to me, if only I may finish the race and complete the task the Lord Jesus has given me' (Acts 20:24, NIV). In pioneer ministry, just as in any other, it is not enough simply to start and set things up well. It is just as important that we finish well, and take whatever steps are necessary to ensure the best chance of our doing so. Paul's experience of pioneer ministry may have been rather more hair-raising than that of most leaders in the present day (see 2 Corinthians 11:24–28), but it undoubtedly remains a challenging and demanding path to follow.

What, then, should we do with the wealth of evidence thrown at us from so many disciplines? Should we, for example, look for pioneering leaders who have no calling whatsoever, and no emotional reaction to the people they care for and support? Of course not! Should we seek people who will accept very poor results and seem perfectly happy with them, in order to avoid falling into the pitfalls of perfectionism? Definitely not!

The key for anyone considering a career in pioneering ministry— or anyone working with pioneering ministers—is much more about developing a very good understanding of the relevant issues about learning who or what to avoid. This level of self-awareness is a vital part of emotional maturity and an essential skill for any pioneer leader. If you choose to work in as demanding (albeit ultimately rewarding) an environment as pioneer ministry, you need to be aware not just of your strengths and the features of your life experience, faith journey and character that have brought you this far, but also of the potential pitfalls or possible weaknesses that those features might also bring.

Perhaps it is fitting to end as we began, with a reminder of the motivation that will drive people on as they enter such a ministry—their calling and passion for the work. This is the energy that will sustain them throughout, whatever the issues they face along the way. In the face of difficult teaching, tough situations and repeated conflicts, many of Jesus' disciples left him. Jesus then challenged his own pioneering team, asking them if they were going to give up as well. Peter's answer was immediate: 'To whom would we go? You have the words of real life, eternal life (John 6:68, THE MESSAGE). Such is the clarity of calling and purpose required for a true pioneer—a clear foundation that will carry them through whatever challenges they face along the way.

Notes

1   For a good example of this, see www.youtube.com/watch?v=lGMG_PVaJoI

2   For example, S.A. Lee, 2009, 'Does empathy mediate the relationship between neuroticism and depressive symptomology among college students?' in *Personality and Individual Differences* 47 (2009), pp. 429–433.

3   C.R. Figley, *Compassion Fatigue: Coping with secondary traumatic stress disorder in those who treat the traumatized* (Brunner-Routledge, 1995).

4   I.M. Cantzler and S. Leijon, 'Team oriented women entrepreneurs: A way to modern management' in *Journal of Small Business and Enterprise Development* 14(4) (2007), pp. 732–746.

5   Cantzler and Leijon, 'Team oriented women entrepreneurs', pp. 732–746.

6   Cantzler and Leijon, 'Team oriented women entrepreneurs'.

7   See N. Harrington, 'It's too difficult! Frustration, intolerance, beliefs and procrastination' in *Personality and Individual Differences* 39 (2005), pp. 873–883.

8   R.A. Baron and D.G. Markman, 'Beyond social capital: The role of entrepreneurs' social competence in their financial success' in *Journal of Business Venturing* 18 (2003), pp. 41–60.

9   D. Abrams et al., 'Innovation credit: When can leaders oppose their groups' norms?' *Journal of Personality and Social Psychology* 95(3) (2008), pp. 662–678.

10 H.S. Khoo and G. Burch, 'The "dark side" of leadership personality and transformational leadership: An exploratory study' in *Personality and Individual Differences* 44 (2008), pp. 86–97.

11 Cantzler and Leijon, 'Team oriented women entrepreneurs'.

12 See B.M. Bass and E.R. Riggio, *Transformational Leadership* (Psychology Press, 2005); J.E. Bono and T.A. Judge, 'Five factor model of personality and transformational leadership' in *Journal of Applied Psychology* Vol 85(5) (2000), pp. 751–765.

13 For example, J. Stoeber and H. Yang, 'Perfectionism and emotional reactions to perfect and flawed achievements: Satisfaction and pride only when perfect' in *Personality and Individual Differences* 49 (2010), pp. 246–251.

14 Baron and Markman, 'Beyond social capital'.

15 J.E. Bono and T.A. Judge, 'Personality and transformational and transactional leadership: A meta-analysis' in *Journal of Applied Psychology* 89(5) (2004), pp. 901–910.

A pioneer's story

For the last seven years, Close House has formed my working environment and has been a major part of my life. Close House is a small charity that provides a safe social meeting space for young people aged 13–25, encourages them to participate in a wide range of activities and offers them the chance to receive deeper levels of individual and group support if they want it. Open each afternoon from Monday to Thursday, Close House is accessed by a large number (300+) of young people who have 'fallen through the net' and are outside school, college or employment. It is also the place from which my call to ordination as a Pioneer Minister in the Anglican Church has come, and a place that has had a major impact on my theology and knowledge of God.

At the heart of Close House are a number of core staff and a large number of volunteers, some of whom are Christians and some of whom are not. They all, however, have a strong empathy with the aim of developing young people as spiritual, as well as physical and emotional, human beings. All the staff and volunteers are encouraged to develop relationships with the young people, building trust and enabling a wide level of support to be given and received.

Over the past seven years I have seen God at work in the lives of so many of the young people attending Close House. I have seen lives saved physically; I have seen youngsters come off drugs, deal with their alcohol problems, stop their criminal activity and bring their violence and anger under control. I have seen them learn to play musical instruments, write their own songs, get involved in photography projects, do film-making, make willow baskets, produce works of art, do a range of 'outward bound' activities and also begin to help as volunteers themselves.

Many 'miraculous' things have occurred in the lives of the young people, staff and volunteers at Close House. One remarkable event concerned the life of an individual who was badged by professionals as having a 'mental health issue'. I am sure he had a good diagnosis and was labelled appropriately, whether bi-polar, schizophrenic, psychotic or depressive. He was part of a 'closed' group at Close House, a peer support group for young people with mental health issues. When he first arrived, I saw someone who was unable to have any kind of conversation with anyone else and was wrapped up in his own world, spending virtually all his time in isolation at home. Over the next six months he was gently encouraged and supported to build relationships with others, and he slowly began to engage with the people around him. We then established that he had been trying to learn to play the guitar, so he was encouraged to become part of a group of young people learning music. Eighteen months after first entering Close House, he performed at a concert, playing acoustic guitar and singing several songs on his own in front of an audience of over 100 people. Some members of the audience were from Mental Health Services, and their jaws were dropping as they saw him perform.

God has been so gracious to us all at Close House, and I have been blessed to be allowed to be part of the work here. It has made me view my walk with God in a different light. Many years ago, my walk was much 'narrower' than today, with a much more restrictive perspective on, among other things, salvation. The blessing I have received from working at Close House includes God's widening of my vision of his work on earth, and I have identified God's influence on many of the non-Christian young people. I have learnt not to constrain God with my own boundaries and perceptions and to be motivated to work far outside the boundaries of the institutional walls of the church. I sense and perceive God's love for all his creation, and can identify with his work in the lives of the abandoned, neglected and abused young people I have the privilege of working with each day.

However, the pioneering venture that is Close House comes with many battles—often, I'm sorry to say, from within the church family, and often because of a narrow perspective on what the work actually involves. Many times I have been asked, 'How many of the young people at Close House have been saved?' or 'When will we see any of your young people at Close House in church on Sundays?' These questions fail to recognise the breadth and length of God's reach and the salvation journey that all of us, these young people included, are on. They also limit the jurisdiction and form of God's saving work, not recognising that the Holy Spirit is at work at Close House, that the love of Jesus is instrumental to the way Close House operates and that all the glory is revealed and acknowledged as God's.

Close House is a new way of being church. Many people, when entering for the first time, say to me, 'We don't know what it is, but we just sense there is something different about this place.' That is a testimony to the fact that God is there and his love is being expressed there. It has been my spiritual home for the last six years and, in all honesty, it is often easier for me to walk through the door to Close House than it is to walk through the door to church on a Sunday morning.

Tony Hodder is the Leader of the Close House Project. He is starting a pioneer curacy in the Diocese of Hereford.

13

The first pioneers: learning from the Acts of the Apostles

Richard Bauckham

Acts is a story of pioneering mission from beginning to end, but, since the most innovative developments occur within the first half of the book, this essay will be limited to commenting on the pioneering elements in the story told in chapters 1—15.

The messianic community in Jerusalem (Acts 1—5)

The first pioneers in church history were the twelve apostles and the large group of other disciples of Jesus who were filled with the Holy Spirit on the day of Pentecost and went on to establish the first 'Christian' community. (At this time, of course, the word 'Christian' had not been invented.) Before this event, they were already, in some sense, a community of disciples of Jesus—people who had taken part in the movement that Jesus himself had led before his death. With the resurrection of Jesus and the coming of the Spirit, however, they were aware that God's purpose for the world had entered a new phase of fulfilment. What Peter preached at Pentecost was that Jesus was now enthroned with God in heaven and had poured out the Spirit on his people so that they should be the messianic people of the last days. Peter and the others did not act on their own initiative when they pioneered the messianic community, and, throughout the narrative of Acts, Luke keeps us aware that the direction and inspiration of every new step that the Christian leaders took came from the Lord Jesus and the Spirit of Jesus. It was, for example, Jesus who chose Paul to take the gospel to the Gentiles (9:15). It was the Spirit who surprised Peter with the unmistakable evidence that Cornelius and his household had been accepted by God without the need for circumcision (10:45–47), and the Spirit who instructed the Christians in Antioch to send Barnabas and Paul on their first missionary journey (13:2–4). These are just a few notable examples of a repeated emphasis in the narrative of Acts on the directing initiative of Jesus. Peter and the others were pioneers on the human level, but only because they took their cue from the Lord and the Spirit.

How did this new community understand itself? Its members were all Jews, of course, and they were not exchanging Judaism for a new religion—far from it. They continued to practise the Torah, God's law for his covenant people, and to worship with other Jews in the temple. Jesus, after all, had done the same. No one would have thought of denying that they were still Jews by practice as well as by birth, but they saw themselves as the Israel of the last days, the nucleus of the renewed people of God, the messianic community of Jesus the Messiah. We can see this in some of the terms they used to describe themselves, all drawn from scripture. They were 'the saints' or 'holy ones' (Acts 9:13 and elsewhere)—that is, the faithful Israel of the last days, as the prophet Daniel had described (Daniel 7:18–27). Their way of being Israel was 'the Way' (Acts 9:2), another term that alluded to scripture. Isaiah had spoken of preparing 'the way of the Lord' (Isaiah 40:3, NRSV) and preparing 'the way for the people' (62:10). The Christian movement was both the way by which the Lord would return to his people and the way by which his people would come to him in the last days. Another Jewish group of the time, the Qumran community, also saw themselves in the prophecy of Isaiah 40:3, but, whereas they took themselves off into the desert to prepare the way of the Lord in sectarian isolation, the Christian community stayed at the heart of the Jewish people—in Jerusalem and in the temple.

The fact that the believers stayed in Jerusalem was no accident or arbitrary choice. They inherited the Jewish sense of the centrality of Jerusalem, where God himself was present among his people in the temple. Moreover, in the Old Testament prophets they would have read of the centrality of Jerusalem for the messianic age. In the last days, all the exiles of Israel would return to Jerusalem, and with them would be the Gentile nations that had also come to believe in the God of Israel (see, for example, Isaiah 60:3–16; Zechariah 8:20–23). Some scholars have supposed that, on the basis of the prophecies, the apostles initially thought they had only to wait in Jerusalem until God brought the returning exiles and the converted Gentiles to them. But the prophecies also predicted that 'the word of the Lord' would go out 'from Jerusalem' (Isaiah 2:3). It is quite likely that the apostles envisaged a worldwide mission from the beginning—something that we also would expect if the risen Christ had given them such a commission, as the Gospels attest.

We often neglect the sense in which the apostles were well placed to reach the whole of the worldwide Jewish diaspora without leaving Jerusalem. Acts implies this when it gives us the elaborate geographical catalogue of the places from which the people came, who were in Jerusalem on the day of Pentecost (2:9–11). It is an accurate sketch of the extent of the Jewish diaspora, from Parthia in the far east to Spain in the far west. On an ancient map, Jerusalem would be right in the centre of this range. There was nothing unusual or surprising in the fact that Jews from all these places were present to hear Peter give the first Christian sermon. Jews from even distant locations came, when they could, on pilgrimage to Jerusalem for the annual festivals in the temple, especially Passover. Several times each year, Jerusalem would be packed with people from all parts of the known world—people who would return to those places, some of them doubtless taking with them the message about Jesus the Messiah that they had heard the apostles preach in the temple courts.

Jews were not the only people who came to the temple to worship. Gentiles also came, especially those who were attracted to some aspects of Judaism and attended synagogues, but without taking the step of actually becoming Jews. If some of these people responded with faith to the message about Jesus, doubtless they took it for granted that they also had to be circumcised (in the case of men) and to observe the Torah, like the messianic community in Jerusalem.

We can easily imagine that, through the constant travelling and communication between Jerusalem and the diaspora, communities of Jewish Christians originated and developed in many places during the early years, when, so far as we know, the Jerusalem church did not send dedicated missionaries beyond Palestine. We know very little about how the gospel reached many of the places in which Christian communities grew up within the apostolic period. In the book of Acts, Luke tells how Paul and his colleagues took the gospel to large areas of Asia Minor and Greece, but he does not intend us to think that this is the whole story of the early Christian mission outside Palestine. He tells Paul's story as *pars pro toto*, one part that represents the whole. He does not expect us to be surprised when Paul, arriving in Rome for the first time, finds Christians there already (Acts 28:15).

Acts 2:42–47 provides a quite detailed sketch of the life of the first Christian community in Jerusalem (with further illustrations of some aspects in chapters 3—5). There are four key elements. Firstly, the whole community gathered in the temple court (probably the only place large enough to hold so large a number) in order to hear the apostles' teaching. At the same time, the apostles preached the gospel to unbelievers, performing healing miracles as signs. Secondly, the believers had 'all things in common' (v. 44). Acts 4:34, 'There was not a needy person among them', alludes to the Torah (Deuteronomy 15:4), suggesting that the practice of community of goods was understood as a sort of creative obedience to the law of Moses. In the messianic age, the Torah's stipulation that there were to be no destitute persons among the people of God should be fulfilled by a radical practice of sharing that went beyond the Torah's own explicit provisions for the poor. We should also remember that many of the members of the Christian community had come to Jerusalem from elsewhere and would not easily have been able to find work. The community of goods was a very practical way of providing for them.

Thirdly, they met daily in private houses to 'break bread' (v. 46), continuing Jesus' own practice of meal fellowship, no doubt with the expectation that he would continue to share his life with them in that way. Fourthly, they attended the public prayers in the temple, which took place twice daily at the times when the priests sacrificed burnt offerings on behalf of all Israel. It is notable that the community's daily life had two geographical foci: the temple and the home. These were already the twin foci of Jewish religion (although, outside Jerusalem, the synagogue would also have played a role), and it may be that the Christian believers' assiduous participation in the daily temple worship especially accounts for the fact that they enjoyed 'the good will of all the people' (v. 47). They were exemplary in their devotion to the God of Israel in the ways that the Torah prescribed.

There is no indication that these Jewish believers in Jesus experienced any tension between the practice of their new faith in Jesus and their continuing practice of God's commandments in the Torah. Since the leaders of the community had been disciples of Jesus during his ministry, we may assume that their observance of Torah was in accordance with the kind of interpretation of it that Jesus had commended in his teaching. This would have set them apart in some ways from other identifiable Jewish groups, but they would certainly not have seen themselves as converts from 'Judaism' to 'Christianity'. Their faith in Jesus was an enhancement of, not a replacement for, their faithful obedience to the God of Israel.

In modern accounts of the early church, the Jerusalem church has sometimes been seen as a sort of incomplete step towards mature Christian faith and practice—a step that soon became antiquated and was superseded. It has even been seen as a reactionary force holding back the progress of the gospel. But this is certainly not how Acts portrays it. For Luke, the Jerusalem church was fully part of, not a mere preliminary to, the story he tells of the success of the Christian mission. This is why he devotes several chapters to it—far more space than he gives to any other specific Christian community. He notes the success of the Christian leaders' evangelistic efforts in Jerusalem, not only initially, on the day of Pentecost, when 3000 believed and were baptised (Acts 2:41), but also subsequently, when the membership of the community reached 5000 (4:4) and continued to grow at an impressive rate (5:14; 6:7). Much later, when Paul makes his last visit to Jerusalem, the elders of the church explain to him that there are 'many thousands of believers… among the Jews', all of whom 'are zealous for the law' (21:20). The Jerusalem church's mission to Jews within Judea had been a great success.

The fact that these Jewish believers in Jesus were 'all zealous for the law' is not a defect, but is just as it should have been. The point is noted because it explains their reaction to rumours that Paul had been persuading Jewish Christians to abandon the practice of Torah. The rumours were untrue, but it is important to note that Paul was not being criticised for failing to require Gentile Christians to be circumcised and keep the law. The issue concerned Jewish Christians. The discussion in the early church as to whether Christians should observe the law of Moses has often been misunderstood because of a failure to distinguish between this issue in relation to Gentile Christians and the issue in relation to Jewish Christians. No one in the early period seems to have doubted that Jewish Christians should continue to observe Torah, as Jesus had done. This was taken for granted. The issue that was discussed was whether Gentile Christians had to become Jews, subject to the law of Moses, if they were to join the messianic people of God.

We shall turn to that discussion shortly, but first a little more needs to be said about the Jerusalem believers' daily attendance in the temple—which has sometimes been understood as a purely pragmatic practice, followed for the sake of the evangelistic opportunities it afforded. This hardly does justice to a practice that earned them great respect among other Jews. But had not Jesus pronounced God's judgment on the temple and prophesied its destruction? Prophecies of the fall of the temple are so well represented in the Gospel traditions that it is not credible that the apostles and others in the Jerusalem church did not know of them. Most probably they reasoned that the temple was indeed doomed but that God would remove it in his own time; until then, while the temple remained, they should continue to participate in the regular worship there. In time, at least, it would be realised that the sacrifice of Jesus made the temple's provision for the forgiveness of sin (as the epistle to the Hebrews argues) unnecessary, but sacrifice for sin was only one of many purposes that sacrifices served.

However, there was one respect in which the temple could present an obstacle to the advance of the gospel. The temple defined the boundaries of the covenant people of God. Only Jews— born Jews or full converts (who, in the case of males, had been circumcised)—could enter the temple proper (the Court of the Israelites or the Court of Women) and participate fully in worship in the holy presence of God. At the limits of the temple space, warning notices threatened death to anyone else who passed them. Gentiles could and did enter the outer court of the temple, which only in modern times has become known as the Court of the Gentiles. They were allowed into this large space because it was not strictly part of the temple, but was a courtyard around the temple. Gentiles could and sometimes did offer sacrifice, but had to do so by proxy. The seriousness with which their exclusion from the temple was taken can be seen in the incident in Acts 21, when a crowd mistakenly supposed that Paul had taken a Gentile into the temple and attempted to lynch him (vv. 27–36).

If the temple defined the people of God, then it was obvious that Gentiles could not join the messianic people of God without becoming practising Jews. The early Christian community in Jerusalem may well have assumed that this would have to be the case, and that the Old Testament prophecies of the conversion of Gentiles to the God of Israel in the last days would be fulfilled in this way. If so, things were soon to change.

Beyond 'the temple made with hands' (Acts 6—15)

Among the pioneers of the next phase of the mission of the early church, as Acts narrates it, was a group known as the Hellenists. Luke introduces us to them at the beginning of chapter 6, as a group within the Jerusalem church who were distinguished from the Hebrews. The two terms refer respectively to people who spoke Greek as their native language and people who spoke Aramaic as their native language (though they might also have spoken Greek as a second language). The Hebrews would have been Jews born and bred in Palestine, while the Hellenists would have been Jews born in the western diaspora (where Greek was the dominant language), who had moved to live in Jerusalem. Many diaspora Jews living in Jerusalem maintained their own identity by having their own synagogues (Acts 6:9). With their Greek mother tongue and their diaspora origins, the Hellenists would probably have shown some cultural differences from native Palestinian Jews and, to some extent, might have had more cultural affinity with Gentiles than did Palestinian Jews. But we should not exaggerate this point. Native Jerusalem Jews had also appropriated many aspects of Hellenistic culture. The assumption, made by many scholars, that the Hellenists might have had a more liberal attitude to Torah observance is probably quite wrong. Most of these diaspora Jews had come to live in Jerusalem precisely so that they could observe Torah more adequately, since only here could they participate in the sacrificial worship of the temple and keep the purity rules strictly. There is no reason why they should have differed *theologically* from the Hebrews in the Jerusalem church. Acts does not suggest that they did. The fact that Paul was a Hellenist (since he was born and raised in the diaspora but later lived in Jerusalem) probably does not explain much about his theology.

Luke narrates the story of the dispute between Hellenists and Hebrews over the distribution of food to widows because it was the occasion for the appointment of the Seven, an event which seems to have been much more important than the situation that led to it. The Seven have often been called deacons, a term that corresponds to the task they were initially given (Acts 6:2), but Acts does not call them by that term and it may be misleading to do so, because the real importance of the two of whom we hear more, Stephen and Philip, was as evangelists. On the basis of their names (v. 5), it seems likely that all of the Seven were Hellenists, although Acts does not explicitly say so. What Luke is really doing by describing the appointment of the Seven is introducing us to another group of leading figures in the church, distinguished from the Twelve, who now become important players in his narrative.

Many scholars have attributed to the Hellenists a theology that, unlike that of the twelve apostles and the Jerusalem church more generally, took a critical attitude to the Torah and the temple, an attitude that would make the Gentile mission possible. For this thesis, Luke's account of Stephen is crucial. Certainly the charges brought against Stephen were that he was committing blasphemy by attacking the Torah and the temple, maintaining that Jesus was going to change the inherited Jewish way of life based on the law of Moses. But Luke makes it very clear that these were false charges (6:12–14).

Brought before the high priest's council, Stephen delivers a speech that has often been read as though it was admitting to the charges, but in fact it is a defence against the charges. It takes the form of a review of Israel's history from Abraham to Solomon. The effect is to portray Solomon's erection of the temple as the fulfilment of God's promise made to Abraham that his descendants would 'worship me in this place' (7:7). The words 'in this place' are not in the Old Testament texts that underlie Stephen's story at this point. They are added (virtually as a quotation from the charges made against Stephen: 6:14–15) to make it clear that the temple built by Solomon was not a mistake or an act of disobedience to God but a fulfilment of God's intention, from the time of Abraham, that his people should worship him on Mount Zion. The rest of the narrative is designed to show how the promise made to Abraham came to be fulfilled by Solomon. Only after making this entirely clear does Stephen add the comment that God 'does not dwell in houses made by [human] hands' (v. 48), citing a prophecy that unequivocally makes this point. The contrast between a temple 'made with [human] hands' and a temple 'made without hands' would have been familiar to Stephen's audience. It was used to contrast the earthly temple in Jerusalem either with God's heavenly temple (directly created by God) or with the messianic temple of the last days, which God was to create as a replacement for the present temple. It is unlikely that any Jew would have denied that the present temple was, in that sense, provisional and temporary. It could not be blasphemy to say so. Thus Stephen refutes the charge of blasphemy while reminding his audience that the temple, though entirely legitimate, is not ultimate.

The charge of blaspheming the law of Moses is likewise refuted by Stephen's account of Moses' reception of 'living oracles' from the angel of the Lord at Mount Sinai (7:38), but Stephen also takes the opportunity of stressing, in this connection, the disobedience and idolatry with which the Israelites greeted this gracious gift of God to them. This enables him, at the end of his speech, to turn the tables on his judges, accusing them of imitating their ancestors in disobeying the law (vv. 51–53). This is the part of the speech that angers them, but even this does not account for their condemnation of Stephen to death by stoning. He has defended himself against the charge of speaking against the law and the temple, but now incriminates himself by reporting a vision of Jesus at the right hand of God in heaven, standing to pronounce judgment on Stephen's opponents. That association of Jesus with God's cosmic sovereignty is the blasphemy for which Stephen is executed.

In Stephen's intentions, his speech had nothing to do with mission to the Gentiles, but, if we ask why Luke has given it so much space in his narrative, the answer probably does have something to do with the Gentile mission. Stephen's speech gives prominent expression to the aspect of the Jerusalem church's theology that enabled them eventually to accept that Gentiles could join the messianic people of God without becoming Jews. Since the existing temple—the temple built by human hands—was, as Jews generally agreed, temporary, and since the messianic age was, the church believed, now on its way, the Jerusalem temple need no longer define the boundaries of the people of God.

Luke's narrative goes on to show how the old boundaries were, in fact, transcended in four stages. Four categories of people who had been excluded from the Jerusalem temple were, one by one, included in the messianic people of God:

1 Samaritans (8:5–25)
2 eunuchs (vv. 26–39)
3 Gentile God-fearers (10:1—11:18)
4 Gentiles (11:19–26; chs. 13—14)

Those who pioneered these new developments were (1) Philip, Peter and John; (2) Philip; (3) Peter; (4) Hellenists, Barnabas and Paul.

They are an interesting mixture of Hebrews and Hellenists, but this development does not represent a split in the Jerusalem church. Two of the Twelve, Peter and John, are as closely involved in these new developments as they were in the earlier narrative of mission in Jerusalem. At the same time, it is notable that the Gentile mission beyond Palestine, actually in Gentile territory, was the work of the Hellenists. (Barnabas, born in Cyprus, was a Hellenist, but one who had been close to the leadership of the Jerusalem church from the beginning. He forms a bridge between the Jerusalem church and Paul, the first evangelist mentioned in Acts who had not been a member of that church at all.) It is not that their theology differed from that of the Hebrews, but that linguistically and culturally they were better equipped for such work.

At every stage, the new developments are mandated by divine action or guidance. There is another interesting aspect, however: as Luke narrates these events, they correspond to biblical prophecy. Isaiah 56:3–8, the passage from which Jesus himself had quoted with reference to the temple (v. 7b; Luke 19:46), predicts that people who were excluded from the temple and thereby from the people of God in the past will, in the messianic age, be admitted to the temple and thereby included in the messianic people of God. The categories of people in the prophecy correspond to the four in Acts as follows:

1 'the outcasts of Israel' (Isaiah 56:8)
2 eunuchs (vv. 3b–5)
3 'the foreigners who join themselves to the Lord' (vv. 3a, 6–7)
4 'all peoples' (v. 7)

With this prophetic substructure to his narrative, Luke is indicating that these pioneering developments, while they took the church's mission beyond the temple, did not take it beyond scripture. Scripture itself indicated that, in the temple of the new age, all would be welcome, with the old exclusions superseded.

Doubtless it was important that no less than the apostle Peter should be the first to allow that Gentiles could join the messianic people of God without circumcision or submission to the whole of the Torah. It was not an easy step for him to take, given the preconceptions he shared with all Jews of his time. He had to be prepared for it by a rather shocking vision in which he was commanded by God to eat creatures forbidden in the Jewish food laws (Acts 10:9–16). The command had to be repeated three times to convince him that God himself, the giver of the law, was declaring these foods fit to eat. Even so, Peter must have been left quite puzzled by the vision, which was designed not to persuade him to abandon the food laws but to work away at his prejudices in preparation for the analogous situation he was about to face.

In a mind educated by the Torah, there was a fundamental analogy between abstention from unclean foods and wariness of Gentiles, whose idolatrous ways could all too easily implicate unwary Jews. By the time Peter enters Cornelius's house, however, the vision has had its effect: 'In every nation,' he declares, 'anyone who fears [God] and does what is right is acceptable to him' (10:35). Perhaps Peter himself has come far enough not to be surprised to witness the Holy Spirit falling on Cornelius and his household when they hear the gospel, but the Jewish believers who accompany Peter are astounded (vv. 45–46). This is the Gentile Pentecost. God makes it unmistakable that the great barrier between Jew and Gentile has finally fallen. These Gentiles plainly do not have to become Jews before they can share in the blessings of the messianic age.

When the news reaches the Jerusalem church, it is not surprising that doubts are raised about Peter's behaviour, but, when he reports the story to the whole church, apostles and other believers, the events prove as convincing to them as they had been to Peter. There is no narrow-minded resentment over the news that God is now sharing with the Gentiles the gift that they themselves have received. Rather, God's generosity with his gifts inspires a generous spirit of praise among the Jerusalem believers (11:17–18).

We might imagine the matter settled, but, with the passage of time, while a mission to the Gentiles outside Palestine, pioneered by the Hellenists from the Jerusalem church and taken up by Barnabas and Paul, got under way and flourished, a minority within the Jerusalem church raised the whole issue again. These 'believers who belonged to the sect of the Pharisees' (Acts 15:5, a phrase which perhaps indicates that they had only recently come to faith in Jesus) began to argue that the Gentiles converted by the preaching of Barnabas and Paul must, after all, be circumcised and take on the whole yoke of the law. The issue had to come to more formal debate and resolution, so a meeting of the whole Jerusalem church was convened.

No more momentous decision was taken in the early church than the determination by the Jerusalem council (vv. 6–29) that converted Gentiles could belong to the messianic people of God as Gentiles. What carried the day were two forms of argument. The first was the evidence of experience, that God was unmistakably giving the Spirit to converted Gentiles. Peter, the first pioneer, very conscious that he had been chosen by God to be the pioneer in this matter, told his story again. Barnabas and Paul added the story of their own corresponding experience with the Gentiles on many occasions during their recent missionary journey. But the case would not have been complete—perhaps not entirely convincing—had not James completed it with an argument from scripture. His carefully chosen text from the prophets (actually a conflation of more than one text, combined in the manner of Jewish exegesis at the time) made precisely the point required to validate the observations of Peter, Barnabas and Paul. It spoke of the time when the messianic temple ('the dwelling of David', v. 16) would be built and the Gentile nations would seek the Lord in it. They are described as 'all the Gentiles over whom my name has been called' (v. 17; Amos 9:12).

The phrase 'over whom my name has been called' is a technical one in the Hebrew Bible, denoting God's ownership, and is frequently used of his covenant people. In this prophecy, the Gentiles, precisely as Gentiles, are called God's own people when they join the Jews in the messianic temple. What Luke does not spell out (but, from the widespread usage of New Testament writers elsewhere, we can presume) is that the messianic temple, the new temple of the new age, is the messianic community itself. At last the story of how the Jerusalem church journeyed beyond the old temple, with its exclusive boundaries defining the people of God in purely Jewish terms, is completed. The new temple in which God dwells in his messianic presence is the messianic community, and God himself has drawn its boundaries precisely by sending his Spirit to indwell the lives of Gentile as well as Jewish believers.

Resources for pioneers

Here are some useful web-based resources about pioneering, for pioneers.

- The Mission Shaped Ministry course from Fresh Expressions is a great training course for pioneers.
  www.freshexpressions.org.uk/missionshapedministry

- Resource offers training weekends each year for people who are living out the call to pioneer new forms of mission. Each weekend is immersed in a different context and explores a particular edge in mission, with a focus on meeting and hearing the stories of local missional communities.
  www.resourcemission.com

- Crucible is a training programme for Christians with courage and imagination, who realise that we live in a mission context and need to think like missionaries. We need to think creatively about church in diverse and changing cultures. We serve the God who constantly does new things on the margins.
  www.urbanexpression.org.uk/crucible/crucible-course

- The Centre for Pioneer Learning provides training, support and networking for all pioneers.
  www.centreforpioneerlearning.org.uk

- Guidelines for the development of lay pioneers in the Church of England.
  www.freshexpressions.org.uk/sites/default/files/
  Encouraging%20lay%20pioneer%20ministry.pdf

- Information about Church Army Evangelists and Pioneers for lay people.
  www.churcharmy.org.uk

- Guidelines for the identification, training and deployment of Ordained Pioneer Ministers in the Church of England.
  www.acpi.org.uk/downloads/
  Ordained_Pioneer_Ministers_Guidelines.pdf

- A short guide to pioneer ministry from Fresh Expressions.
  www.freshexpressions.org.uk/sites/default/files/
  ExploringPioneerMinistry_2.pdf

- Information about the Methodist Church *Venture FX* for lay and ordained pioneers.
  www.methodist.org.uk/index.cfm?fuseaction=opentoworld.
  content&cmid=2539

- A list of various Church of England institutions that provide training for Ordained Pioneers.
  www.freshexpressions.org.uk/training/related/opm

- Some MA postgradute courses on mission.
  www.freshexpressions.org.uk/training/related/postgraduate

Here are some books on pioneer leadership:

- Dave Gibbons, *The Monkey and the Fish* (Zondervan, 2009).
- Angela Shier-Jones, *Pioneer Ministry and Fresh Expressions of Church* (SPCK, 2009).
- Tim Keel, *Intuitive Leadership* (Baker Books, 2007).
- Alan Roxburgh, *The Missional Leader* (Jossey Bass, 2006).

Growing Leaders

Reflections on leadership, life and Jesus

James Lawrence

Seven out of ten Christian leaders feel overworked, four in ten suffer financial pressures, only two in ten have had management training, and 1500 give up their job over a ten-year period. At the same time, as financial restrictions affect the availability of full-time ministers, more people are needed for leadership roles in local congregations, for every area of church work.

This book faces the challenge of raising up new leaders and helping existing leaders to mature, using the model for growing leaders at the heart of the Arrow Leadership Programme, a ministry of the Church Pastoral Aid Society (CPAS). It comprehensively surveys leadership skills and styles, discerning our personal calling, avoiding the 'red zone' of stress, developing character, and living as part of the community of God's people.

With a foreword by Bishop Graham Cray.

ISBN 978 1 84101 246 9   £8.99
Available from your local Christian bookshop or, in case of difficulty, direct from BRF using the order form on page 223. You may also order from www.brfonline.org.uk.

Messy Church®

Fresh ideas for building a Christ-centred community

Lucy Moore

Messy Church is bursting with easy-to-do ideas to draw people of all ages together and help them to experience what it means to be part of a Christian community outside of Sunday worship.

At its heart, Messy Church® aims to create the opportunity for parents, carers and children to enjoy expressing their creativity, sit down together to eat a meal, experience worship and have fun within a church context.

The book sets out the theory and practice of Messy Church and offers 15 themed programme ideas to get you started, each including:

- Bible references and background information
- Suggestions for 10 easy-to-do creative art and craft activities
- Easy-to-prepare everyday recipes
- Family-friendly worship outlines

ISBN 978 1 84101 503 3   £8.99
Available from your local Christian bookshop or, in case of difficulty, direct from BRF using the order form on page 223. You may also order from www.brfonline.org.uk.

Messy Church® 2

Ideas for discipling a Christ-centred community

Lucy Moore

Following the popular *Messy Church* formula, *Messy Church 2* not only provides a further 15 exciting themed sessions, but also explores ways to help adults and children alike to go further and deeper with God—in other words, to grow as disciples.

As before, the material is overflowing with ideas for creativity, fun, food, fellowship and family-friendly worship, but new to *Messy Church 2* are 'take-away' ideas to help people think about their Messy Church experience between the monthly events.

Across the year, the 15 themes explore:

- Loving God, our neighbours and our world
- The life of Jesus: growing up
- Bible women: Ruth, Hannah and Esther
- Christian basics: who God is
- Baptism: belonging to the family of God
- Holy Communion: sharing and caring together

ISBN 978 1 84101 602 3   £8.99
Available from your local Christian bookshop or, in case of difficulty, direct from BRF using the order form on page 223. You may also order from www.brfonline.org.uk.

Ministry Rediscovered

Shaping a unique and creative church

Mike Starkey

In this book, Mike Starkey sets out a compelling vision for how local church ministry can involve a call to creative thinking, to stepping 'outside the box', rather than labouring to work with standard assumptions about congregational growth and models of what constitutes success. Drawing on his own experiences and insights from a wide range of contexts, from inner city to rural, he offers challenge, guidance and encouragement for all those answering the demanding—and at times exhilarating—call to serve the Church.

ISBN 978 1 84101 616 0   £7.99   Available from October 2011
Available from your local Christian bookshop or, in case of difficulty, direct from BRF using the order form on page 223. You may also order from www.brfonline.org.uk.

The Challenge of Change

A guide to shaping change
and changing the shape of church

Phil Potter

Change can feel uncomfortable and risky, but it is an ever-increasing force in society. Decisions on what and how and when we change will inevitably affect growth or decline in a church, and will also have a major impact on people. Leaders can end up burnt out by their attempts to bring about change, or by facing up to the challenge of it, while congregations are left damaged and disillusioned because they could not catch the vision.

This book offers a map for healthy and godly change. Writing as a pastor and practitioner, Phil Potter explains ways of shaping all kinds of change in the life of a church, particularly in the context of the fresh expressions emerging. This is a book for leaders who want to take their congregations through change, and for church members wanting to be equipped for whatever lies ahead. It speaks to reluctant traditionalists and impatient visionaries, to both struggling and thriving congregations. Also included are over 100 questions for personal and group reflection.

ISBN 978 1 84101 604 7   £7.99
Available from your local Christian bookshop or, in case of difficulty, direct from BRF using the order form on page 223. You may also order from www.brfonline.org.uk.

Word and Spirit

The vital partnership in Christian leadership

Will Donaldson

The Bible—the Word of God—and the Spirit of God are inextricably bound together, as the story of God's working throughout history reveals. The Word tells of God's unfolding purposes for the salvation of his world, and trains us in godly living. The Spirit inspires and illumines the text and fills us with power and gifts for ministry and mission. Sadly, 'Word' and 'Spirit' have become increasingly identified with divergent parts of the Church, impoverishing our witness and weakening the body of Christ.

This book calls Christians to focus on what unites rather than divides, and to come together in a celebration of both Word and Spirit to build each other up and further the sharing of the gospel. It not only traces the shaping of this 'vital partnership' through Christian history, but explores their shared importance in key areas of church leadership and ministry.

ISBN 978 1 84101 825 6   £8.99
Available from your local Christian bookshop or, in case of difficulty, direct from BRF using the order form on page 223. You may also order from www.brfonline.org.uk.

ORDERFORM

REF	TITLE	PRICE	QTY	TOTAL
246 9	Growing Leaders	£8.99		
503 3	Messy Church	£8.99		
602 3	Messy Church 2	£8.99		
616 0	Ministry Rediscovered	£7.99		
604 7	The Challenge of Change	£7.99		
825 6	Word and Spirit	£8.99		

POSTAGE AND PACKING CHARGES				
Order value	UK	Europe	Surface	Air Mail
£7.00 & under	£1.25	£3.00	£3.50	£5.50
£7.01–£30.00	£2.25	£5.50	£6.50	£10.00
Over £30.00	FREE	prices on request		

Postage and packing	
Donation	
TOTAL	

Name _____ Account Number _____

Address _____

_____ Postcode _____

Telephone Number_____

Email _____

Payment by: ❑ Cheque ❑ Mastercard ❑ Visa ❑ Postal Order ❑ Maestro

Card no [ ][ ][ ][ ] [ ][ ][ ][ ] [ ][ ][ ][ ] [ ][ ][ ][ ] [ ][ ][ ]

Valid from [ ][ ][ ][ ]   Expires [ ][ ][ ][ ]   Issue no. [ ][ ][ ]

Security code* [ ][ ][ ]   *Last 3 digits on the reverse of the card.   Shaded boxes for
ESSENTIAL IN ORDER TO PROCESS YOUR ORDER   Maestro use only

Signature _____ Date _____

All orders must be accompanied by the appropriate payment.

Please send your completed order form to:
BRF, 15 The Chambers, Vineyard, Abingdon OX14 3FE
Tel. 01865 319700 / Fax. 01865 319701 Email: enquiries@brf.org.uk

❑ Please send me further information about BRF publications.

Available from your local Christian bookshop.   BRF is a Registered Charity

Guidelines

Bible study for today's ministry and mission

Guidelines

Bible study for today's ministry and mission

Regular Bible reading and study should be at the heart of the spiritual lives of anyone involved in ministry, whether as a minister, lay reader or preacher, or as a member of a leadership team. Sometimes it is difficult to find a way of making that Bible reading and study happen in a manner that is challenging and engaging, while still making the all-important link between personal faith and ministry.

Guidelines, BRF's Bible reading notes for those looking for in-depth study, with its focus on ministry and mission, is an ideal resource to give church leaders confidence in reading the Bible and using it to equip their ministry.

Published three times a year (January, May and September), this series of notes offers the flexibility of readings in weekly or daily portions, by a variety of contributors. Each set of readings has an introduction, comments on the designated Bible passages, and a weekly 'Guidelines' section with points for thought, prayer, reflection and action. *Guidelines* is suitable for individual use or group study, so why not make it part of your ministry team's regular programme?

Guidelines is available from your local Christian bookshop or by subscription direct from BRF.

Visit www.biblereadingnotes.org.uk for further information, including details of the PDF download version and the iPhone and iPad app.

About

BRF is a registered charity and also a limited company, and has been in existence since 1922. Through all that we do—producing resources, providing training, working face-to-face with adults and children, and via the web— we work to resource individuals and church communities in their Christian discipleship through the Bible, prayer and worship.

Our Barnabas children's team works with primary schools and churches to help children under 11, and the adults who work with them, to explore Christianity creatively and to bring the Bible alive.

To find out more about BRF and its core activities and ministries, visit:

www.brf.org.uk
www.brfonline.org.uk
www.biblereadingnotes.org.uk
www.barnabasinschools.org.uk
www.barnabasinchurches.org.uk
www.faithinhomes.org.uk
www.messychurch.org.uk
www.foundations21.org.uk

If you have any questions about BRF and our work, please email us at

enquiries@brf.org.uk